TEACHING SUCKS

but we love it!

A little insight into the profession
you <u>think</u> you know

FRANK STEPNOWSKI

outskirtspress
DENVER, COLORADO

Praise for *Why Are All the Good Teachers Crazy?*

"...there's a reason why, if you enter 'Teacher' under books on Amazon. com for the last 3+ YEARS, you would find **Why Are All the Good Teachers Crazy?** in the Top 10—clearly, the truth contained within its pages continues to resonate with people that can handle it."

–Ryan Schoenwolf (Pennsauken, New Jersey.)

"Finally, a look into what really goes into teaching the kids that not a lot of people want to teach. Frank tells it like it is."

—Kevin Czapor (Limerick, PA)

Funny, heart warming, great insight and so well written. Don't let the title fool you, there is much to be gained by <u>anyone</u> who reads this book.

—Charles Grone (Dacula, Georgia)

As a teacher, I'm a tough critic and very cynical about books written about the teaching profession. I find most of them cute and heartwarming...but I rarely find them realistic in nature. **Why Are All the Good Teachers Crazy** was a breath of fresh air. I am grateful to read a book that tells the true trials and tribulations we, as teachers, go through everyday just to maintain some sort of order."

—Maria Frey (Swedesboro, New Jersey)

"To say that Frank gives us a fresh look at education would be a huge under-statement. I read most of this book while on hall duty at school. Teachers and students would stop to ask me why I was crying/laughing/crying/shouting AMEN!"

—April Estep (Peytona, West Virginia)

"This book saved my teaching career. Teaching can sometimes feel like an impossible task and it can often leave you feeling desolate and alone. Frank's book makes you realize that you are not the only teacher feeling around in the darkness."

—Samantha Abbot (Whale Cove, Canada)

"Our dad asked us to say something about his book. It's got a green cover, teachers seem to like it, but it's not like it got him on Oprah or anything."

—Samantha, Mason and Frankie (the author's children.)

Praise for *S.C.R.E.W.E.D., An Educational Fairytale*

"Incisive, insightful, moving and terrifying…for all its fierceness, the message of the book is surprisingly practical and gentle."
— Frank Wilson: **The Philadelphia Inquirer**

"A funny and honest look at the educational system."
—Tom Waring: **The Wire**

"Its narrative is a fantasy world for teachers, imagined by one of their own… extremes and shock value aside, S.C.R.E.W.E.D. outlines some rather simple, yet elegant, fixes."
—Matt Brannon: **The Spirit**

"Although allegorical in nature, Step's ideas seem not too far off the horizon, given our current educational climate and state of the country as a whole. The education of America's youth is a complex, multifaceted endeavor, and… [the author] makes a valiant and skillful attempt to address all of these facets, all while keeping the reader thoroughly entertained, from start to finish."
— Dr. Jason Secoda (Philadelphia, Pennsylvania.)

"The author delivers the TRUTH with blunt force. This book was written in the trenches…If you are involved in Public Education at any level, you need to read this book."
—William Snyder (Pennsauken, New Jersey.)

"I haven't read it, but people tell me it's very funny."
—Dawn Stepnowski (the author's wife.)

Dedication

Dawn
You kept me from committing suicide many, many years ago, and you've
probably kept me from committing homicide many times since then.
In all the space between, you've worked tirelessly to allow me to parent,
teach, write, and live the only way I know how.
You are the only role model strong enough for our daughter, and you make
it easy for me to show our sons how to love a woman unashamedly.
I have hurt you too many times, and you have endured the worst of me
while simultaneously bringing out the best in me.
You have complicated my life beyond my comprehension; and yet,
you have simplified my life in the only way that matters.
While *you* and *I* may not see eye to eye on most things,
that which we do agree upon make **US** a very powerful force indeed.

"I will not be commanded. I will not be controlled, and

I will not let my future go on without the help of my soul."

—Greg Holden *The Lost Boy*

Table of Contents

Introduction
By Demons Be Driven
and Guided by Gods.

Certain people wouldn't shut up, and certain people wouldn't speak up, and so someone had to step up. The demons that drove me to write this book were myriad; in fact, you could say that they are all heads of the same hydra—the educational system:

- Out-of-touch politicians who pass laws and promote programs (sometimes for their own financial gain) that negatively affect people whom they have no desire to know or to live anywhere near.

- Spineless administrators who, in the name of $elf pre$ervation, enforce, without question, the aforementioned laws and programs, even to the obvious detriment of the students they swore to help. (MOMENT of CLARITY: As I write this, it occurs to me that many of these administrators, who knowingly "stick it" to their constituents and sleep like babies because they secure their jobs by doing so, are being well trained to be future politicians.)

- Self-involved (or simply uninvolved) parents/guardians who overcompensate for their behavior by enabling their children and promoting the type of ignorant, antisocial behavior that made *them* such winning role models.

- The offspring of these parental train wrecks who, ultimately, become our students. Kids that not only don't want to learn, but also *celebrate* their [willing] stupidity and ignorance as badges of honor.

And finally,

- Those lazy, uninspired teachers who give some small shred of credence to the aforementioned heads of the hydra spewing their colossally uninformed (yet all-encompassing) anti-teacher vitriol.

  Quick question: What do all of these haughty hydra-headed hags and has-beens have in common?

  Quicker answer: They all feel perfectly comfortable spouting off publicly *and* privately about why teachers are underworked, overpaid, and responsible for everything from the failures of their precious children to the downfall of Western civilization.

  Another quick question: Why don't the GOOD teachers fire back and defend themselves, and the *good* students they work with?

  Another quick answer: A lot of reasons: maybe they're afraid of being fired, maybe they know that Mark Twain was right when he said that "A lie can travel halfway around the world while the truth is still putting on its shoes," <u>or maybe they're just too busy filling every moment of their day doing their jobs as teachers and parents the *right* way</u>.

  There could be any number of reasons why good, hard-working teachers don't hit back.

  But guess what?

One did,

and that's the reason for the book you're holding in your hands.

Of course, this whole business of book writing isn't something one embarks upon lightly. In fact, one very astute 5th grader inquired during a "meet the author" thing I was doing at a Middle School in New Jersey—*"don't you feel more pressure writing books now that people read your other ones and know who you are?"*

Damn, kid, when you put it that way…

In truth, his was a brilliant question that warranted consideration. I did, indeed, feel a LOT more pressure this time around. The shocking success of my self-published writing debut and the media coverage/controversy that accompanied my second one certainly made me feel I had something vaguely resembling a reputation to live up to in starting a book that many people (both inside and outside the education field) were actually **waiting** for.

Crap.

I'm not that good.

No, seriously, I read *CONSTANTLY*, and I *teach* Literature. I've even been invited to participate in a few author roundtables, so I know what great authors sound like, and *I ain't one of them.*

So, about a third of the way into this, as I sat and tried to organize my inane ramblings into a coherent book worth reading, those voices that so often offer clarity in moments of distress came calling, and none of them were encouraging, believe me.

Those nasty voices almost led me to scrap the whole project, but salvation came in the form of Joseph Campbell, writer and lecturer, best known for his work in comparative mythology and religion. The man was a genius, and that is not a term I use lightly.

I have taught Campbell's <u>Monomyth</u>, also referred to as *The Hero's*

Journey, a 17-step cyclical plotline, to legions of students. They ALL tell me that it opened their eyes to how every adventure story "follows the same pattern" and how those same stories always relate back, ultimately, *to our own personal journeys through life.*

You see where this is going, don't you?

Without getting all "English-teacher-y" on you, I saw how *my* adventures, as a teacher, could readily apply to anyone grappling with our current educational system, be they teacher, substitute, student, parent, administrator, etc. because, to quote Ashford and Simpson, "I'm every woman, it's all in me."

So I figured I'd do what I do best.

I complained and ate pizza,

but THEN I got down to the business of teaching and writing.

I'm going to give you the super quickie version of "the journey" and then we'll get started. For purposes of this book, I'll be the hero. *(I can hear you laughing from here and I am deeply wounded; just go with it, ok?)* If it makes you feel better, insert Hercules, or Luke Skywalker, or Mulan, or The Hobbit, or...oh, you get the point!

With apologies to Joseph Campbell; here is, for your reading pleasure ,the super-quickie-Step-version of the Monomyth:

1. **The Call**—Starting off from humble beginnings, the hero receives a call to start his adventure.
2. **Refusal to leave**—Duty, obligation, FEAR, or something else makes the hero hesitant to venture into the unknown.
3. **Supernatural Aid**—Heroes almost always get some sort of "magical helpers."
4. **Crossing the Threshold**—The hero leaves his home, heading into a world unknown (or at least very dangerous) to him.
5. **Belly of the Whale**—Our hero is "in it to win it" now, having finally separated himself from the comfort zone.
6. **Road of Trials**—All those adventures, tests, antagonists and trials along the way. (Note: The hero is probably going to fail at some point during this phase of the journey.)
7. **Meeting with the Goddess**—The hero encounters an unconditional love that keeps him going in the face of failure.
8. **Temptation**—The hero is tempted, in any variety of ways, to stray from the path.
9. **Atonement with the Father**—Our hero must confront whatever holds the ultimate power in his life.
10. **Apotheosis**—The (usually metaphorical) "death" of the hero, necessary for him to "take it to the next level."
11. **The Ultimate Boon**—The BIG ACHIEVEMENT of the goal. Of course, the journey always becomes about more than the *original* purpose, so this is NOT he end...
12. **Refusal to return**—He didn't want to leave, but now, having seen so much, the hero doesn't want to go home.
13. **Magic Flight**—that mystical "kick in the pants" that speeds the hero back to where he needs to be.

14. **Rescue**—Usually exhausted, wounded, etc. our hero often needs to be helped/guided to the "finish line."
15. **Crossing the Threshold (Back)**—Time to come home, carrying the vast amount of knowledge he earned by surviving the journey.
16. **Master of Two Worlds**—Ah...balance between the spiritual and material worlds.
17. **Freedom**—And isn't that what we're all looking for at the end of the day?

And so, driven by demons but guided by the Gods, book 3 took shape and found its way into your hands. Enjoy; and, if you feel in any way vindicated, empowered, or comforted by *my* journey, look me up and let me know; I'd love to hear about *yours*. —Step

PART I
THE CALL TO ADVENTURE

Wherein our hero starts off in a situation of almost painful normalcy *until* some information comes to him that acts as a call to head off into adventure.

My adventure started in Dunkin Donuts, and it led to the writing of a third book that I swore I'd avoid like the plague.

Soundtrack for this chapter: *My Love Will Not Let You Down*
—Bruce Springsteen

I Would Die for Your Kid.
12/14/2012 and 9/11/2001

I had just left work for the day, the entire weekend was ahead of me, and although I had a ton of work to do, I was looking forward to my Friday ritual: hard work out, hot shower, sit for a half hour and reflect …

before the "*can you drive me to* (insert location,)" or "*can you pick me up from* (insert sport practice)," or the "*we need to* (insert time consuming activity) this weekend…" began.

Those of you with kids and a spouse and a life know what I mean.

I stopped at Dunkin Donuts to pick up the traditional cup of pre-workout rocket fuel, when I glanced up at the television screen and saw the report on the killings that had taken place at an elementary school in Newtown, Connecticut. As I watched parents collapse in grief, and read that many of the victims were *children*, I stood, mouth open, processing the freezing fear that was birthed in my stomach like some malignant animal.

My man Vishnu, the guy who provides me with large coffee and small talk almost every day, waited, very patiently, while I stared for I don't know how long at the horror unfolding in front of me. When I snapped out of it, he just handed me the coffee and nodded, sadly, recognizing my grief. It wasn't until I made it home (a 10 minute drive I don't remember at all,) that I realized he didn't charge me.

As a teacher, and a father of four, I feel compelled to discuss this most heart wrenching tragedy, in the hopes that if I talk about it, I may be able to scab up the reopened psychic wound that previous school shootings have left on my soul. If at all possible, I may also be able to find one shred of light amid what is almost inconceivable darkness.

Before I go any further, let me acknowledge, and pay the highest respects to, the heroic women that made all of us proud to be educators, and humbled to be mentioned in the same breath: Dawn Hochsprung—principal of Sandy Hook Elementary School, who ran selflessly towards the sound of gunfire in an effort to help the children she swore to protect. School psychologist Mary Sherlach, who also died putting herself in harm's way, and first grade teacher Victoria Soto, who literally gave her life *for* the little ones she had already, metaphorically, given her life *to*. These women will remain eternal symbols of all that is best and boldest about our profession, and it is only fitting that they remain iconic among the teaching community for reminding the world that **our** impact on **their** kids extends far beyond the classroom.

That having been said, I know that a lot of the people I teach with would, without hesitation, put their lives at risk to defend the same students that sleep in their class, curse them out, ignore their advice, and fail to do their homework, and you can count me among them. Nowhere in my contract does it say "and will put himself between an active shooter and his students…" but I refer to my students as "my kids" (even when I am *formally* discouraged from doing so) so I would *treat* them like my kids if push came to shove.

And I am not alone.

I think the halfwits that continually bash teachers in the media would do well to remember that.

They would also do well to remember that we, the teachers, are very often the ones talking to your children about the stuff they don't feel comfortable talking to *you* about. Our influence cannot be denied, nor can our importance be overestimated, as we often know your kids better than you do.

I know that's a hard pill to swallow, believe me I do, I'm a parent myself, but **the fact is, the modern teacher is educator, disciplinarian, psychiatrist, surrogate parent, counselor, clergyman, confidant, storyteller and friend.** They don't teach you how to do any of that in college, I assure you.

You know what else they don't teach you? How to comfort a group of children when a terrorist attack on your soil happens while you're in front of the classroom.

Flashback to September 11th, 2001. I was teaching Shakespeare; I remember that because I was told "you can't teach *those* kids Shakespeare." Ah, the "experts"… I do so love proving them wrong. *Those* kids, by the way, were a dozen 16-18 year old young men who had perpetrated any number of crimes and misdemeanors to wind up in my class in my former school. They were "bad kids," "criminals just biding their time until they wound up in jail," "society's incorrigible;" I heard it all.

And so did they,

and they thought the people saying it were as full of it as I did.

Anyway, I was teaching *Hamlet* (check out my first book for the full, hilarious details) and my buddy and fellow teacher Gabriel Oke excused himself and told me "dat a plane had crashed into one of de Twin Towahs."

*NOTE: I have written about my dear friend from Nigeria in both of my previous books, and it has become a prerequisite that I "write like Gabe speaks;" to the point that, when I see Gabriel in person, he does **me** doing **him**. It's freakin' hilarious.*

You have to remember, this was going down *live*, and none of us had any idea what was to come, so I simply suggested that, although it was very peculiar, there had to be a logical explanation: the pilot had a heart attack or something. Gabe went back to his classroom (and the only TV on "campus") until he returned a few moments later, and with grave seriousness beckoned me to the door. "Step... anuddah plane struck de uddah Towah."

And thirteen young men that were **never** quiet went mute.

Fast.

"What does dis *mean*, Step?" inquired Gabriel, who seemed to sense (based on his body language) *exactly* what it meant. Now it was up to us, with no time for rehearsal, to engage two classrooms full of children **(I don't care what they did in their lifetimes, they were still KIDS)** in a moment that we were pretty sure that we would all remember for the rest of our lives. Lives which, in that moment, seemed very precious indeed.

One more time for emphasis, folks: They don't cover how to handle terrorist attacks or psychotic people with assault weapons in the collegiate teaching curriculum.

So let me ask you—you are fairly certain that terrorists are launching attacks on your home soil, which may trigger a *much bigger* threat; your 5,4, and 3 year-old kids are 20 miles away *across a bridge in another state*, and you're in front of a room of severely emotionally disturbed students. What would YOU say to a room filled with *very* impressionable, *extremely* volatile, *potentially* violent teens [with abandonment issues?] You have NO time to think about this.

Go.

For my part, I went with a strategy that has, oddly enough, worked every time I've employed it, regardless of the age, type, or class of students—I told the truth.

"OK, guys, I am pretty sure that we just got attacked by another country. I do not know how this is going to go down, but as I find out any credible information, I will tell you. The first thing I am going to do is check in with the principal and see what the plans are; while

I'm doing that, see if you can arrange rides. One thing I can tell you for certain—I am going to get my kids, but I will not leave any of you alone to do that. I love you too much to do that, no joke, but don't even **think** *about hugging me. I can fit all of you in my truck, and if I have to drive you all home one at a time, I'll do it. [Screw] it, if you all have to crash at my house, so be it, but I'm getting my kids, and you're welcome to come with me. You can help me keep them from being scared.*

You in?"

They were in. Looking back on this moment many times over the years, I have gone over what I said and whether it was "right" about a million times. I've consigned myself to the fact that I did a pretty good job shooting from the hip.

Of course, that is a byproduct of spending time in front of the classroom and having to "wing it" in the face of chaos. EVERYthing, from the honesty, to the profanity, to the humor, to the "I will not leave you alone," to the idea that THEY could be the source of comfort *to someone else* were calculated to elicit strong reactions, put them at ease, and empower them in the face of uncertainty and fear.

I thought about this moment again when I saw the interview with first grade teacher Kaitlin Roig, who during the unfolding massacre in Connecticut, told her elementary school students: *"I need you to know that I love you all very much"* because *"[she] thought that was going to be the last thing they were ever gonna hear."* Sadly, she felt the need to qualify her actions, claiming that she *"was not sure if it was appropriate for a teacher to tell her students that [she] loved them but [she feared] [she]was going to be killed along with the children."*

At that _precise_ moment in time, without even realizing it, **I heard THE CALL.**

But before I digress, allow me to answer that question:

Yes, Kaitlin, it is ALWAYS appropriate to tell your students that you love them. If you mean it, and they will **_know_** if you do, it is the

<u>single most powerful thing you can do for them,</u> (and it will facilitate learning with a nuclear-grade capacity.) I am embarrassed on behalf of my species that we are creating an educational system where ANY good teacher feels torn at the idea of expressing authentic emotion, particularly when an ever-increasing number of our kids come to school emotionally vacant, thanks to the deadbeat/absentee parents that blame teachers for the lack of empathy within their children (that *their* lack of quality involvement, more than any other factor caused.)

I am a teacher,

and I would die for your kid.

You would do well to remember that.

Now that *your* eyes have been opened and *my* ears have "heard the call" to move forward; there are a few other things you should know about teaching, why it sucks, and why we (the good teachers) love it anyway…

PART II
THE REFUSAL OF THE CALL

Often, when he hears "the call," our future hero refuses to heed it; this may be a result of some sense of duty, an obligation to others, a feeling of inadequacy, or just plain fear.

How about E) *All of the above?* I was already spending enough time away from my family doing my *regular* job the right way. Plus, I didn't want to let down the people who read the other books with a half-hearted effort. Finally, I was just scared—scared that I couldn't adequately explain the daily agony of being a teacher to anyone outside the profession, scared of a lot of things...

Soundtrack for this chapter: *Supremacy of Self* —Hatebreed

Elephant in the
Eye of a Needle

Interesting;

I'm fired up now. Got a million ideas for book 3, even decided to write this one *sans potty mouth* (not easy for me) so the message gets out to the general public—the ones that think they know what teachers deal with every day.

But now I'm scared.

HOW do I get the non-teachers out there to understand the minutiae and B.S. that wear down the modern teacher without boring them with page after page of "talking shop?"

Seriously, how can you explain to someone *not* in the profession, who's inundated by all the anti-teacher rhetoric all over the media, about something like the nightmare scenario of standardized testing without confusing the hell out of them or boring them to tears?

You can't.

So why put myself though the agony of writing, editing, paying to publish, trying to promote, and enduring the criticisms of, a book that would change about as many minds about teachers as a visceral Facebook post changes peoples' minds about politics?

Why indeed?

I was suddenly afraid to start something that might disappoint the people that [I was delusional enough to believe] were counting on me.

(Note to Mr. Spielberg, when you're directing the cinematic adaptation of my life, this is me, filled with pathos, refusing the "call to action," *yet knowing full well that I'm full of crap and that I'll do it anyway.*)

Luckily, it only took a few conversations [about education] with friends and strangers alike, to make me re-realize that it only takes a few facts to make folks stop and reconsider their previously held prejudices and beliefs about teaching (usually because they were only repeating something they were *told*.) That having been said, I know that—if you're reading this, you fall into one of four categories:

1. You're a teacher, or you work in education.
2. You're a friend or family member of a teacher/person that works in education.
3. You read one or more of my previous books.
4. (possibly all of the above,) OR
5. Someone wonderful and deserving of a hug recommended this book to you.

If you're in one, or all, of the *first three* categories, you probably know SOME of the stuff in here (although there may be some unpleasant surprises even for you.) However, you might lack the patience, time, or clarity to "break it down" to others who pass judgment based on scraps of [mis]information they glean from the *compleeeeeetely unbiased* media (Insert wicked, *I'd-Mortal Kombat-fatality-them-if-I-could-get-away-with-it* laughter here.)

So your old buddy Step is here to provide a quick primer of just a few of the things that make teaching in the modern era suck harder than a Dyson vacuum on steroids. For example:

- **Did you know** that, in many districts, your child's failing grades, including zeros, are "rounded up" to 50s or 60s?

- Speaking of grades, **did you know** that the minimum passing grades are being lowered so as not to jeopardize graduation rates? I personally know of one school where a *58* is rounded up to a 60, which is considered a passing "D."

D for d-ploma, I guess.

- While we're on the subject of grades, **did you know** that many, MANY students with tons of absences (some of them unexcused) "earn" passing grades by sitting in "credit restoration" sessions? That's right, a kid that missed 20+ days in, say, a "College Prep" English class can put in a few hours staring at the walls, in a classroom, after school, (like an extended detention *with no educational component whatsoever,*) and not only pass the class **but be allowed to take College Prep English next year.**

Of course, EVERYbody is (in name only, trust me) College Prep now…

- Oh yes, **did you know** that course titles are being changed and students are being homogenously grouped together so that the people running the schools can claim *"we have x number of college prep and honors classes, blah blah blah;"* basically denying that there are average or, heaven forbid, below average kids, in anything—frustrating the kids that *don't* belong in there and watering down the education of the ones that *do*?

And speaking of lose-lose scenarios…

- **Did you know** that it is becoming almost impossible to suspend or expel a child from school [for anything short of premeditated mass murder] without towers of paperwork, months of waiting and expensive, time consuming, legally gridlocked manifestation hearings? Meanwhile, those children (that are "entitled to an education") remain in school, *knowing* they're on borrowed time, and behave in school in ways that would get them arrested on the street; distracting teachers, scaring kids, and—again—watering down the education of the good students.

- And **did you know** that one of the *reasons* it's so hard to get rid of the miscreants that are gobbling up your tax dollars, watering down the decent children's education, and *who don't want to be in school right now in the first place* is because everybody has some sort of 'diagnosis' now? In fact, it has become PROFITABLE for public schools to diagnose kids with things like ADHD and such! Do some research—you'll be amazed [and infuriated] with what you find.

- Since the watering down of education seems to be a trend here, **did you know** that Big Corporation leaders have been gushing like teenage girls in love about the new Common Core standards* being employed in schools. *Meanwhile, those same "rich folks" send their kids to private schools* that will probably ignore those standards! Think long and hard about that if you're not independently wealthy. And, if you're reading this book, you probably aren't.
  *Common core = the stuff we're TOLD to teach, more on that later.

Speaking of reading…

- **Did you know** that, in school across the country, reading is *supposedly* being "prioritized" while budgets for books and libraries are being CUT by as much as HALF? And that some of the tests students are forced to take to assess their reading levels are sponsored by publishing companies that recommend only *their* books at the conclusion of the tests?

- **Did you know** that the MANDATED pursuit of data collection has superseded actual teaching and that the MANDATED drudgery of forcing kids to take standardized test after test after test has replaced actual learning? **School has become a place where** (take a deep breath and repeat after me)—**the students are taught to <u>pass tests </u>by *teachers* who are being told they will be fired** (if the kids don't pass) **by *administrators* who are threatened with replacement** (if those teachers don't "do what they're told") **by *politicians who are* funded, which is to say *owned* by *Big Business CEOs* who don't have a clue about real education** (but know *for a fact* that <u>THEIR KIDS WON'T BE ATTENDING THE SCHOOLS WHERE THIS SINISTER CRAP IS *MANDATED!* </u>)

Oh yes, the people who run this country looooooove benchmarks, standardized testing, common core standards, data collection and manipulation and one-size-fits-all schooling for kids…

Your kids,

not *their* kids.

Their kids will be going to private schools that do not give standardized tests and will likely ignore the common core.

And while we're on the oh-so-touchy subject of alternatives to public education, let me drop some knowledge on you about the uneducated population's FAVorite solution to the failing public school system—Charter Schools!

- **Did you know** that charter schools are, for the most part, *public* schools, *funded by taxpayers;* hence they are promoted like public school—you know, "open to everybody." That's a LIE. All across the United States, charter schools "weed out the undesirables" based on such things as: academic records, parental support, disciplinary history, motivation (however THAT is assessed, I don't know,) "special needs" and, in some cases, legal citizenship; which is, by the way, a violation of *state* and *federal* law.

Oh, but they're so successful!
Uh…not really.

1. **News Flash:** If I was allowed to *hand pick* every kid I wanted, my little league baseball team would kick ALL of your asses, too, but that's because I know how to teach and care about my "players." Unfortunately…
2. **News Flash part deux:** Even though they ARE allowed to hand pick their "teams," MANY charter schools—gasp!—fail miserably.

Which is a major disappointment to some very interesting people…

- **Did you know** that, under a federal program known as EB-5, wealthy foreigners can basically *buy U.S. immigration visas for themselves and their families* by investing at least $500,000 in "certain development projects." I'll give you *sahn* guesses what some of those development projects are…

Oh, I could go on and on, and I haven't even *touched* the dead-beat, enabling parents and lazy, uninspired teachers yet.

But I will.

Rather than bore you with statistics and redundancy, I'll simply break it down like this: The quality of education for your children is being compromised at a dangerous rate, and it's not going to stop unless people wake up, START paying attention and STOP blaming teachers for everything simply because WE ARE THE ONLY PEOPLE **CLOSE** ENOUGH TO YOUR CHILDREN TO **RESPOND** TO YOUR COMPLAINTS.

Wake up, people. Good teachers (and, for purposes of discussion, I'll put myself in that category) don't do this job because we want kids to hate school, lose their sense of accountability, and pass some arbitrary test(s) that will only be changed next year to keep everyone dancing in circles;

and we sure as heck don't do it for the *money*.

I don't make a penny off of the **billions** spent "negotiating" what publishing company provides the textbooks, what business services the technology, or what corporation provides the food services in our schools, nor do I care.

I just teach your kids, no matter what books they read, computers they use, or food they eat.

I teach them to think, to be socially appropriate, and to have a sense of decency and accountability. I teach them to read between the lines and **QUESTION EVERYTHING**, so they don't blindly follow the increasingly controlled "education" that teaches them only WHAT to think, WHEN to think it, and WHO to listen to. I teach them to feel good about themselves even if, *especially* if, they're not good at the very narrow list of things that modern, compulsory schooling says is "important."

I teach your kids because I love them.

Yeah, I said it.

I love them.

Not in a *let's-all-hold-hands-and-sing-Kumbaya* sort of way, more of a *you-along with <u>my</u> kids—will-inhabit-and-shape-the-future-of-the-world-those-I-love-will-be-living-in-**so-I'm-going-to-care-for-you-as-I-would-my-own-children** sort of way.

Not all teachers feel that way, and those who don't should get out of the profession.

Now.

But *you're* smart enough to know (once you've taken a few moments to get to know us) which are which. So take those few moments, **get to know the people who have almost as much influence on your kids' outcomes as you do,** then do a little research on some of the things I mentioned earlier and some other interesting things you may uncover about your child's education.

In the meantime, please,

PLEASE, stop voting down school budgets, and/or telling me "teachers only work for 9 months;" and think about how you would do things differently if the people in charge at *your* job weren't so clueless and out of touch.

Understand, above all, that I'm fighting my arse off for your kid,

in many ways,

both inside and outside the classroom.

So please stop fighting me while I'm fighting for you.

And if you're fighting the good fight, trying to really educate our children, peers and fellow citizens amidst a rising tide of toxic nonsense,

if you feel alone, and that nobody understands what you're going through; **know that I wrote this book for you**, so cut me some slack if I didn't get to everything you wanted me to cover, because this was like trying to fit an elephant though the eye of a needle.

PART III
SUPERNATURAL AID

Once the hero has committed to the quest (and *that*
didn't take long, did it?) his guide(s)/ magical helper(s)
appear in one form or another.

Too many people to mention help me do everything I do, but this particular
literary venture took the shape it did thanks to an eponymous source of
inspiration.

Soundtrack for this chapter: *Come to My Aid* —Simply Red

Opus Eponymous

OK, I had heard the call, given myself every excuse to REFUSE it, shot them all down, and finally started doing all the author-type stuff I do when I start writing a book. I was on my way...

right up until I hit the wall.

It was too toxic, you see, this ever-increasing pile of stuff I wanted to write about. I KNEW people wanted to hear about it, you could see evidence of it everywhere. Social and print media were flooded with stories about:

- Teachers being forced to hate the profession they love, while their out of touch overlords bent over and assumed the position for their political leash holders.
- The "high stakes" testing inflicted upon our kids *increases*, while our kids' ability to think (in ways absolutely necessary in the current global economy) rapidly *decreases*.
- Meanwhile, a Facebook page titled *"Just Let Me Teach"* gets almost 3,000 "likes" in a month.

...methinks there might be a message in there somewhere.

So, like one of my students, I sat staring at a blank laptop screen.

My advice to them is "just start writing SOMEthing and the ideas will start flowing" so I typed out the words *The System Sucks*. No kidding; great revelation there, Step. Then I typed *"Everyone thinks they know what it takes to be teacher, but they **don't**."* Yeah, you're setting the world on fire now, Step. Punched out *"Teachers need someone to speak up for them, do NOT be afraid to make enemies by telling the truth."* Sounds like a mission statement, but better than nothing. In frustration, I typed out something so profane that my laptop almost caught fire. Embarrassed, I finally attacked the keyboard one last time and promised *"absolutely no profanity this time, do not wallow in negativity,"* *"offer hope"* and *"don't confuse the readers, educate them!"*

I looked at my first few "brainstorms" and compared them to my self-imposed guidelines and came to the logical conclusion:

I was an idiot, and this was hopeless.

Because this time, I was feeling it, front and center. It's very hard to ignore the war when you're in a hot zone, and I was watching, every day, *good* parents, students, teachers, etc. getting crushed under the wasteful nonsense that passes for education these days. I watched self-serving administrators fatten their resume's and completely incompetent educators get promoted simply because they were the right race, gender, demographic, pay scale, *or they were simply compliant enough to do whatever they were told,* even to the obvious detriment of the children they were sworn to educate.

Good. Now you're angry, too;

and you understand, a little, why I couldn't start writing.

With 105 new students, all (as any teacher will tell you,) less prepared, more lacking in social skills, needier yet more resistant than ever, along with 4 children of my own (all involved in myriad activities because I'm trying NOT to be like the deadbeat parents I have grown to loathe,) a marriage to maintain, and the tsunami of "other stuff" that manages to fill the cracks of anything resembling what we used to remember as 'free time," well,

I didn't have much time to write.

And when I did, I just couldn't inflict the toxicity (from revisiting all the things I was angry about) upon myself again. I was neutralized by negativity, drowning in depression, and...uh, anesthetized by anger.

OK, got a little carried away there.

This was ridiculous. I even had the *title* for the book ready to go— *Why Are All the Good Teachers Crazy* ANGRY. It was perfect. My first book, *Why Are All the Good Teachers Crazy* still, after three years, sells like hotcakes, so just change the title up a little bit, play to the crowd, and Bam! instant book sales. Only one problem...

I don't WRITE for the %^$#!@? money.

I write *"[because] writing a book is a horrible, exhausting struggle, like a long bout of some painful illness. One would never undertake such a thing if one [was] not driven on by some demon whom one can neither resist nor understand."* —George Orwell: prophet, literary genius, author of books WAY better than this one, said that.

He's right, you know.

But I just couldn't bring myself to start writing, even though I couldn't shake the feeling that, beneath the nuclear winter of all this academic devolution, there was hope.

There's always hope.

I see it, I feel it, and I hear it, in the words, actions, and day to day grind of students, educators, parents and people that *care*—and I am one of them. I care so much that, at the risk of hyperbole, it threatens to rip me apart sometimes, and the grinding, Conan's wheel consistency of that caring has made me consider leaving the profession that I was **born** to do. How then, could I perform the necessary verbal assault and battery on the idiots that deserved it while still putting forth a message of real, tangible, BELIEVABLE hope, in a book called *Why Are All the Good teachers Crazy* ANGRY?

I couldn't, and that's why it took so long to start writing again. I tried reading authors I admired, talking to teachers that inspired, gathered some focus groups and inquired, and yet nothing transpired. (…got a little carried away again; it happens.)

Of course, inspiration need not come from "outside" sources; indeed *out of the mouths of babes oft times come gems.* Enter my youngest son Frankie.

Somehow, between football, baseball, track, working, helping out around the house, pulling straight As, not cleaning his room, and earning Playstation 3 awards on *Black Ops*, he manages to find time to hang out with his dear old dad and engage in some quality conversation.

I truly enjoy those moments.

I came into my office and found young Francis reading stuff from my "why do I do this?" folder. Basically, I have a big expanding file folder filled with letters, cards, printed out Emails, etc. from parents, students, teachers, readers, etc. that I go to in those dark moments when I doubt everything I do and wonder why the hell I remain a teacher when I could make a lot more money doing something far *more* respected and far *less* time consuming.

- That happens a lot, and the folder helps; A LOT.
- I recommend <u>you</u> keep a "why do I do this" folder, whatever your "this" may be:

Back to Frankie who, with feet up on my desk, glanced at me over the top of a letter like a professor looking at a student who was late for office hours. *"Did you read all of these?"* he asked.

"No, what do they say?" I replied, in a snarky tone that said "well, you got your one stupid question of the day out of the way."

"ACTually," he continued, undaunted, *"some of them are pretty amazing. "*

He put them, neatly, back into the folder and, looking right at me, locked eyes, and paused for dramatic effect (I taught him *too* well) and then reminded me, quietly:

"Some of those people that read your books…you really helped a lot of them. Some of my teachers read them and said they were amazing. Teachers need you. They're afraid; you're not. You always say we have to protect people. You need to write another book about teaching."

"Teaching sucks, Frankie."

"Yeah, but you love it;" he smiled, *"now write another book."*

And on his way out he added:

"Soon."

Your wish is my command, son, now until the day I die.

The simple words of a young man, free of prejudice, ulterior motive or fear, provided the clarity and purpose I had been looking for, and all the motivation I would ever need.

Flesh of my flesh, blood of my blood—YOU are my supernatural aid.

PART IV
CROSSING THE FIRST THRESHOLD

At some point, the protagonist must actually cross
into the field of adventure, leaving the known limits
of the world he understands and venturing into an
unknown (and dangerous) realm where the rules and
limits are unfamiliar.

Once the decision was made to start the writing process again, I felt the old
feelings coming back: the rage, the indignation, the frustration, the passion,
the pain—all amazing in their own way. The wicked satisfaction of knowing
you've pissed off all the right people. The sheer joy that comes from knowing
you've written something that will make at least one person pump their fist
and say "Yes, me too!"

The cathartic release of putting yourself out there for the whole world to
read.

The fear and exhilaration of writing about a journey where the ending was
still uncertain

Away we go.

Soundtrack for this chapter: *Been Away Too Long* —Soundgarden

My Job Is To Teach Them *With* You, Not Raise Them *For* You.

The title of this chapter alone ought to tell you that I have "<u>crossed the threshold</u>" <u>with extreme prejudice</u>, and I have no intention of going back until this is done.

WARNING: Let's get this out of the way before we even pass GO and collect our $200, because if you don't like what I have to say *here*, well…To continue the Monopoly metaphor, this chapter is the purple properties with no houses on 'em. The REST of this book is like landing on Boardwalk with *two* hotels crammed on it.

Still want to play with me? Then roll the dice and away we go.

I hear a lot of talk about "why the kids [in this country] are failing:"

But EVERY SINGLE chart, statistic, and spreadsheet I am forced to look at, EVERY SINGLE news story, documentary, and YouTube rant I am encouraged to watch, EVERY SINGLE factoid, scale and statistic I am choked with in the ever-growing, steaming pile of "student data," EVERY SINGLE one leaves out *one* important factor;

one very, VERY important factor.

Ironically, this factor tends to have the most to say about *my* effectiveness in teaching *their* kids.

Did I give it away?

Richard Steele observed that "the rudiments of education are given, very indiscreetly, by most parents," and he was right. The problem is—and it's a BIG one—that most parents think it my job, as a teacher, to teach their kids everything from basic common courtesy to advanced literary awareness, and everything in between.

News flash, folks: *It's my job to teach them* **with** *you, not to raise them* **for** *you.*

Also from our breaking news department: You do NOT get to take your frustrations at feeling like an inadequate parent (which we ALL feel from time to time) out on *me*.

Just because YOU can't—with every factor possible at your disposal and the *other* 23 hours of the day, weekends, two months in the Summer and the preschool years before he got to me—control your kid, don't even DREAM of blaming me for your fragile, illiterate, angry little ball of enablement when I'm armed with only 45 minutes a day and ever-shrinking resources.

I am working my tail off, in spite of everything, to educate your children and create a better world for them, and I would love your help in doing it. I'll even take your constructive criticism and input, provided we can talk like adults and agree to disagree on things. I understand you're passionate about your kid.

So am I.

But I will not tolerate your disrespect, nor will I tolerate "parent-approved "disrespect from your child. As I told one particularly prickly parent, who accused me of having "messed up" her child's education: "You drove the car for 16 years before I got it, I didn't break it during the test drive."

She didn't like that. Asked me "what [I was] trying to say."

I told her "I wasn't *trying* to say anything; I was *explicitly saying* that she had a hand, a BIG one, in the 16 year-old product she was accusing me of ruining in approximately 21 classroom hours.

She didn't like that, either.

Want to know the best part? The KID in question LOVED my class, and sat in the meeting trying to disappear into his chair while Mommie-not-so-dearest proceeded to thrust HER agenda onto her clearly more evolved (and tolerant) offspring.

I would love to tell you that little *intercambio de palabras* was an isolated incident, or that THAT was the worst story you're going to hear in this chapter, but we both know that's a far cry from reality.

In fact, I could tell you stories about parents that:

- TOLD their children NOT to do assignments that were given in class,
- Stood in offices yelling at teachers that they [the teachers] were hurting their children WHILE THE CHILD IN QUESTION CRIED AND BEGGED THEM TO STOP
- Told their children ON THE PHONE (not allowed) IN CLASS, that they DIDN'T HAVE TO LISTEN to the teacher

…and so much more.

And I'll bet dollars to doughnuts that if you know someone who is a teacher, they could tell you a handful of stories just like the ones I mentioned (or worse.) The sad reality is that this "adult" (and I use that word *very* loosely) posturing is creating hyper-sensitive kids who don't know WHAT they stand for, and who can't fight their own battles when they *do* find something to stand for.

No surprise that we have a generation of kids who are statistically unprecedented in their LACK of *ability* but ABUNDANCE of *entitlement,*

which is a shame,

…especially if you have to teach them.

What, I ask you, is a teacher to do with a kid who has been told his whole life that he is great at everything (when he isn't,) *but is reading on a 4ᵗʰ grade reading level in 11ᵗʰ grade,* and then tells *ME* that his step-dad told *HIM* that reading *Flowers for Algernon* was "gay?"

How about the little girl who listens to her mom bad mouth her teacher (to her friends during one of their extended *whine-about-something-you-know-nothing-about-but-never-actually-DO-anything-about-it* sessions) and **then** tells her 4ᵗʰ grade teacher "I don't have to listen to you, and my mom says you don't know $#!+ about what you're doing?"

Both true stories;

and, unfortunately, more and more common.

Tell me—what are we supposed to do?

Parents, largely because they have been enabled by conflict-allergic "school leaders," have a license to yell at, scream at, insult, degrade, question, usurp, deny, mock, challenge, ignore, *slander* and over-rule teachers (sometimes to the extent of getting them reprimanded, fined or fired.)

But if I teacher so much as *implies* that maybe a **parent** needs to be more involved with a child that—take a deep breath and read this—*has a list of discipline referrals longer than his arm* (including sexual harassment, profanity and threats toward teachers, and open defiance,) *is failing multiple classes AND has missed several days of school* (during which *nobody at his house* could account for his whereabouts?!?)

If a teacher even *implies* that maybe that **parent** shares the responsibility for that child's failure as a student and a citizen…*Jihad upon the teacher!* (Often with the backing of a spineless administration that will coddle and cajole the angry "parent" the same way the "parent" did to their little future statistic.)

Again, **true story.**

Again, more common than you dare to believe.

Mind you, this same "parent" has never shown up for a back-to-school night or parent-teacher conference, sends back 'work to be signed' unsigned, *won't* provide an Email address, *CAN'T* provide a phone number (that won't change every other week,) and has—if you do a little research—blamed a LOT of people prior to you for the underachievement of their child.

This is the equivalent of getting in your *third accident,* in a car you were *given, without a license or insurance,* and *suing everyone else on the highway* for your damages; and I've witnessed this lack of accountability in every district and from every demographic imaginable.

I would say that these people should be put to sleep or prevented from breeding any further, but I would never suggest such a thing, as that is the realm of stand-up comedians and politicians.

Scathing sarcasm aside, let's get back to some real-life stories, shall we?

Yesterday, as I was editing a different chapter, a story came on the news about a school in Penns Grove, New Jersey where a teacher was accused of racism for a project she gave to her class. According to the story, a "well respected, well liked teacher of many years" was accused, "by one parent" of being racist because "she gave her *special education class* an assignment," (after reading the book *NightJohn,)* where they were able to "choose being an abolitionist or a slave owner, then write a persuasive essay and design a poster" from the point of view of their chosen side.

The parent in question refused to be identified (shocking) and a COMMITTEE was formed *to speak for* him/her at the BOARD MEETING (which included the Superintendent, school board, union reps, and members of the undefeated 1972 Miami Dolphins football team.) OK, I made some of that up, but the point is that ONE complaint, from ONE parent, that did not necessarily reflect the opinion of their ONE child, led to a committee being formed, at least one board meeting convened, and enough wasted man hours to pay for at least a new computer or two for that special ed. class.

What I DO know is that this is becoming common practice as educational personnel scatter like cockroaches when the light comes on to prevent one minute of face-to-face communication about the suddenly soapbox-worthy beliefs of one individual whose volume-to-civility ratio is dangerously out of balance.

Counter-productive cowardice, pure and simple.

I've got a better idea:

1. Parent—call or Email the teacher and explain your offense, *in the same civil tone you would expect your child to employ were he/she involved in a workplace dispute.* (Teacher, you may, of course, take the initiative and call first.)
2. Allow said teacher to explain his/her rationale.
3. Perhaps, heaven forbid, **get to know each other**, apologize for any miscommunication, agree to work for the best of the kid, come to an agreement or, on occasion, agree to disagree.

Do NOT make it unbelievably awkward for that child to return to the classroom by turning **your** issue into a media circus or a scene from a reality show. In short, treat the person that offended you *like you would want to be treated,* were the roles reversed.

"Do unto others as you would have them do unto you."

Somebody should put that in a book somewhere.

I think it bears repeating that the allegedly racist teacher had been a well-respected, and well liked, teacher with nothing in her past that would in any way indicate racist behavior. Why, then, wasn't the teacher given the benefit of the doubt [by the parent and their "community activist" mouthpiece] that anyone else in a similar situation would have been afforded? I think it has a lot to do with the increasing hostility toward teachers that seems to be permeating the landscape, which we will talk about in more detail later, I promise.

HAPPYADDENDUM:

I am very pleased to report that the district Superintendent, Dr. Joseph Massare did, in fact, (as of the writing of this chapter,) support his teacher and give her the benefit of the doubt, saying that she "was totally proper and followed appropriate educational material." Bravo, sir.

SADDENDUM:

On the very day I went back and added the aforementioned **happy** news to the book, I had the following **sad** encounter in a WaWa right around the corner from my school.

So, I was at WaWa grabbing coffee. (This is a reoccurring theme, folks; my *blood type* is black coffee,) and I noticed a young man with his mother waiting for their lunch orders to be filled. Interestingly, I had just passed through the front office on my way out the door, stopping to ask the secretaries if *they* wanted coffee, too—

(Say what you will about me, people, but I know the right posteriors to kiss.)

—and I saw the same young man and his mother coming out of my 'deer' friend Mr. Venison's office. Now, when a student and a parent are coming out of the principal's office holding paperwork, the parent looks angry and the kid is looking at his shoes, that usually means SOMEbody received an out of school suspension.

Bingo.

On my way past them, I pieced together enough of the VERY heated one way conversation (done entirely in Spanish) to know that the young man—let's call him Moishe, for irony's sake—had cursed out a female teacher and *since this wasn't his first time* he was suspended for a few days; and mom was hotter than a Mexican-Israeli ghost chili.

Or so I thought.

Moishe and mom sure *seemed* a whole lot chummier waiting for their convenience store quesadillas than they were not 5 minutes prior. They were now speaking perfect Ingles', so I understood per-fect*ly* that the whole display in the front office was just that, a display.

This is the conversation as I heard it, verbatim. NOTE: anything I wasn't sure of I left blank, but I wrote it down as soon as I got back to my truck, knowing it would be useful for the book.

"You know how them white folks is (nino ?) -------- for sure. They just don't know. That [expletive] can't handle her [expletive.] These teachers is (crazy/lazy?) anyway.

She asked him to grab some plastic forks; and he was telling her that he would probably have a lot of makeup work to do [upon his return] and, as she was telling him that ***"you ain't doing no damn makeup work and you best not get [punished] for it. They put you out that's their problem..."*** he spotted me looking directly at him.

Ignorant maybe, but stupid he was not, and he went over and said something under his breath to mom.

Have you ever had somebody NOT look at you so intentionally that it seemed like you were the only two people in the universe for those few moments?

Yeah, it was something like that.

Silent as I walked past them, she resumed (albeit in a slightly dif-ferent tone) as I paid for my coffee.

"You might had your reasons, Moishe, but you can't just be cus-sin' people out, you know? Now you gonna have to do work and apologize to that lady."

I heard that clear as a bell, mainly because it was said so I <u>could</u> hear it. So I returned the favor. "You know why I just get coffee and never eat the food here?" I asked Jeanne, the older woman behind the counter.

"No hon, why not?"

"Because it's **artificial**."

And I looked right at Moishe's mom when I said it. She continued to not look at me, but Moishe saw me, and looked down every time I passed him in the hallway for weeks after his return (until I finally pulled him aside and talked to him about the awkwardness of the situation, the nature of accountability, and how the Spurs were going to win the NBA championship.)

What? Well you can't be *all* business *all* the time, now can you?

Mom and I never got to speak, which is a shame, but her actions illustrate just another example of what I'm talking about. How the heck are we, as teachers, supposed to instill any kind of accountability in the kids we teach when we have parents not only *condoning* rude, threatening, ignorant behavior but, in some cases, *encouraging* it?

Which brings me to my final story for this chapter:

Sometimes, you have to, as my friend Dennis says, "go above and beyond above and beyond" in this business. Any decent teacher, sub, counselor or school nurse knows exactly what I'm talking about. Sometimes, however, "above and beyond to the 2nd power" just isn't enough. Sometimes, the algebraic equation of enabling parent + non-accountable kid = frustration on a Grand Canyon-esque scale.

Had a student, 17 year-old male named Vincent Furniay (pronounced fur-nee-ay) who told me on the first day of school that "[he] *didn't want to be called Vince.*" Mind you, he told me this as I encountered his legs (which he had stretched out, with his feet up on another desk, blocking me from getting down the aisle.) *"Call me by my nickname—Duro. It means hard in Spanish."*

Never was there a more ironically nicknamed child.

"Duro" was white, with not a trace element of Spanish in his bloodline; furthermore, he was, in reality, softer than a mouse pissing on cotton in a padded room.

My guess is that the pseudonym was self-awarded, but social violations aside, I had already been given fair warning about "Duro" from a host of other staff members who had dealt with his particularly annoying brand of passive-aggressiveness (and subsequent enablement from his aunt, who we'll get to in just a bit.)

Most of the comments went something like *"Oh, you got VINCENT, well, he'll probably be ok for you, but wait until you call home"* or *"You're gonna love this kid, he'll lie, cheat, and fail, then make up stories about you not being fair;"* etc.

Needless to say, Captain Cottonelle did not disappoint. Vincent was one of those kids that thought you were picking on him after you finally wrote him up after you told him thirty times to put the phone away in class. You know the type.

Of course, poison apples often come from poison apple trees.

Which brings us to Duro's auntie.

Less than two months into school, Mr. Furniay submitted an assignment that was so painfully obviously plagiarized that I thought, rather than get upset and offended, I would make an example of how impossible it was to get such shenanigans past your smarter-than-the-average-bear English teacher. I would let him re-do the assignment because, hey, maybe nobody ever taught this kid about plagiarism.*

*I know what you're thinking. The kid made it to Junior year of *High School* without being educated on plagiarism? Stranger things have happened, believe me.

So I highlighted the plagiarized parts, and wrote the website he got them from (and there were seven different ones) next to each answer. I caught him before he entered the class, showed him, and told him to get it signed. On the bottom of the paper, I wrote a note to his aunt, expressed no malice, but asked permission to use the assignment to educate the class about how easy it was to ascertain plagiarism. I told her [that I had told him] that he could re-do the assignment the right [honest] way for full credit now that he had learned his lesson.

I got back a signature and the words "OK" scrawled next it. Duro made it a point of telling me, *in front of the class*, that his aunt had laughed and told him "he didn't need to re-do the assignment, he had all year to make up that grade."

I chose not to use the assignment, and to let the comment pass. I became resolved years ago to the fact that some parents want you to teach their children all of the things they never got around to, but to do so without any criticism, correction, chastening or chastisement.

Sure, and while I'm at it, I'll sculpt something beautiful out of this granite block using just a Q-tip and a Sham-wow.

But I digress... suffice it to say that I suspected Auntie Maim might, (despite her enthusiastic "you GO, Mr. Step" responses to my monthly update Emails) turn out to be that particular brand of canine that, having lived under your roof for years, bites you the one afternoon you forget to feed it on time.

Twas' in the chilly days of early November, frost on the pumpkin, and 2nd marking period coming to a lackluster close for Duro, when I forgot to feed the dog on time.

I had been Emailing, texting, and calling Aunt Akita to no avail to let her know about the ever mounting evidence that her rather flocculent nephew wasn't doing so well. Based on past experience, I assumed that:

A) Maybe she was just tired of hearing bad news (perfectly understandable,)
B) she was, as a single woman raising kids, extremely busy; (very possible and very admirable,) or
C) the messages were being intercepted and deleted prior to arrival. I've been down *that* road more times than I can count.

(Can't say *I* wouldn't have tried that if answering services existed in my youth.)

D) Or maybe there were other issues I could assist with or keep my nose out of, thank you very much.

So I sent the following Email.

Ms. Akita,

I've sent you a few Emails, a text, and waited for you at parent-teacher conferences (*Duro told me you weren't responding because you'd "get all caught up" there*) but I have received no replies of any sort. Super busy? Not interested? Your nephew deleting them before you get 'em? Other? Please let me know so I know how to proceed from my end.

—Step

Mind you, the last time I "spoke" to this person she was cheering me on for my approach to teaching, so I allowed myself to believe (despite my suspicions) that we had a rapport going.

Silly rabbit.

I received a reply within MINUTES of sending my Email, which I thought was a *good sign*.

(I know, I know… I'm face palming right now in hindsight of how misguided I was.)

I shan't go into too much detail, but the highlights included: calling me *"ridiculously stupid,"* telling me to *"be a teacher not a preacher,"* demanding that I *"manage"* and referring to me as *"very highly opinionated with a big ego."*

Uh…ok. Not sure how we got all that from a 63-word inquiry, but this wasn't my first

E-assault from a parent. After I recovered from the surprise at the visceral nature of the oft-misspelled reply, I responded:

Ms. Akita,

First of all, at no point did I question the importance of your nephew's education to you, and I saved ALL of my previous Emails, and your responses, as proof of that; in fact, I have done nothing but respond to *your* request to keep you informed...

Furthermore, I have encountered *many* cases of Emails being deleted, messages being erased, etc. in my years as a teacher, and you, yourself told me that Vincent hasn't told you the "whole truth" about certain things in the past—*so I was not, as you implied, "stupid;" rather, I was trying to ensure that you were informed.* Vincent's grade point <u>average</u> for the entire 2nd marking period was a 59, so mine is clearly not the only class he is under-performing in; I just wanted to keep you abreast of *why* that was the case from my end.

You chose to take that personally for reasons beyond my comprehension, as I have done nothing but be honest and accommodating to both you and your nephew. For you to refer to my suggestions as *stupid*, accuse me of preaching anything, *and then presume to pontificate about my character* is unacceptable.

I will not "manage" anything, <u>what I *will* do is talk to Vincent and his counselor about transferring him out of my class, as you</u> (with your response) <u>and he</u> (with his continuing lack of accountability)<u> have put me in a position where I can no longer be objective about him, let alone be as accommodating as I have been up to now.</u> I'm sure, given your obvious opinion of me, that you'll agree that this is for the best.

—Mr. Stepnowski

Believe me when I tell you, I was more hurt than angry, but I made a decision a long time ago that I would do everything and anything for my students, including (and it hurts to say this) sometimes taking time away from my own kids in the process. However, I have *never*, nor *will* I ever, allow parents/guardians to slander or bully me in any way, shape, or form.

I think Ms. Akita sensed that and, to her credit, seemed to *want* to resolve the issue; however, passive-aggressiveness seemed to take precedence over sincere apology, and I was told, in another quick response, that *"she couldn't take back how she interpreted my words or what she said"* **(actually she could, but...)** and that I was *"always shining light on [my]self."* **(Whaaa???)** She also closed with letting me know that *if I wanted to give up that easily on Vincent* **(you're kidding, right?)** *she couldn't stop me, as I had control over who was in my classroom* **(since when?)** *but that it was disturbing that we, as adults, couldn't agree to disagree* **(I thought that's exactly what we *were* doing.)**

At this point, perhaps I should have cut my losses, listened to the legions of administrators, counselors, and fellow teachers that had dealt with this individual, and just indulged 'Duro' and his immaturity/ lack of academic effort for the rest of the year. The problem was, Vince was starting to become a distraction to the other students I was trying to teach (and, to be honest, they were a bunch that didn't need any additional distraction.) Furthermore, I wasn't going to just walk away without setting the record straight on the litany of incorrect assumptions that had been attributed to me. Finally—and most importantly—I have to walk the walk to back up the talk I talk to my own kids, whom I have repeatedly told that sometimes, to put an issue to rest, you must apologize even if you think you are in the right. That having been said...

Ms. Akita,

Agreeing to disagree is *exactly* what we are doing. I completely understand one's passion regarding one's children, but I emphatically disagree with the manner in which you responded to a simple inquiry toward someone who seemed to be, (based on our previous correspondence,) a kindred spirit. Please allow me to address some of your comments in order:

You said you can't take your words back, nor should you, if you truly believe what you said about me, but I can't figure out if you do or not. You claim to have never questioned my dedication, yet you *immediately* said that I am *"giving up"* on Vince? Your responses to my monthly Emails were always emphatically supportive, yet you *repeatedly* referred to me as *"shining light on [myself?]"* You ask me to keep you informed, yet you respond with *insults* and *accusations* when I ask you basic questions based on YEARS of previous experience AND your own nephew's commentary?

Bottom line: You went from "AMEN!!!!" in your last Email to calling me stupid, egotistical and willing to "give up" on a student in this one. I really thought we were on the same page, *but if you truly find me that base and self-serving, why would you <u>want</u> your son subjected to me any longer?*

<u>I do, sincerely, apologize</u> for taking our kinship for granted in that I thought I could shoot you a quick, lighthearted, Email asking how you wanted me to move forward, any offense or implications were *absolutely unintended,* <u>and I am sorry</u> and surprised that you didn't automatically know that; but your responses were personal, uninformed, and uncalled for. Finally, you were dead wrong about two things: I have NO say in who is in my classroom, but *your* input is invaluable to your nephew staying there. We both know Vincent has a history of discipline problems AND doing poorly in English classes; that makes my having to "get with him" (again) at some point almost inevitable. Up until now I thought I was moving with the backing of a supportive guardian who understood my methods, but now I wonder if I have to concern myself with you taking everything I do personally. If so, then this class is not the best, most therapeutic learning environment for him, and I will, per professional protocol, seek another placement. If we're cool, he stays, we move on, agreeing to disagree on some things, but unified in our desire for the best education for your nephew. —Step

I received a very moving, [what I thought to be] heartfelt response from Duro's aunt apologizing profusely for taking her frustrations with him out on me. She ended by saying she was too embarrassed to say any more but that I could "continue safe in the knowledge that [I]had [her] support."

That was on a Tuesday.

That Friday I assigned the class a Persuasive essay in preparation for the state mandated HSPA tests coming up within a few days. I made it crystal clear that this was a very important, and very personal, assignment that HAD to be done by Monday.

On Monday, Vincent was the *only* student out of fifty-one (including two young men that KNEW they were failing for the year but did it anyway because they knew it was personally important to me) that didn't submit an essay.

NOTE: I didn't realize this until *1am Tuesday morning* as I finished grading the last one.

On Tuesday, outside of class, I asked him about it and was told that "my aunt said I didn't have to write no essay like this 'cause I felt some kinda way about it." Suddenly, I was back to my childhood, trying desperately to pack soft, powdery snow into something resembling a useful snowball. It didn't work back then, either.

On *Friday* I was informed (after barging into the counseling office like the Terminator into Sarah Conner's house) that snowball had been transferred out of my class *Wednesday morning* and that this move had been made at the suggestion of his aunt and approved by his counselor, the grade-level vice principal and principal.

I was, to put it mildly, pissed.

In a quarter century of teaching, I have only lost two students (and by "lost" I mean transferred into a class identical to mine of the same level in the same building) and I blame myself explicitly for the fact that they transferred out of my class during an active school year.

I know, I know...I should have been happy, right?

Should have been *thrilled* that Mr. Charmin Ultra-Soft and his Auntie Bipolar were no longer going to be contributing factors to my ever-problematic blood pressure;

should have been even *more* ecstatic that his seat was filled [within 2 business days] with a young lady I had previously taught as a 9th grader (so she entered the class with a great work ethic and was elated to be there;) thereby replacing a hemorrhoid with a warm summer breeze, AND **VINDICATING** my promise that if any student chose to leave, *their seat would be filled the next day.*

Should have been on Cloud 9, this was a win-win right?

Wrong.

I have always been very proud of the fact that I—like most good teachers—promise to take *whatever* students are given to me, in whatever *situation* they are given, and teach them like my life depends upon it, often with pretty damn good results. So I consider it a professional failure on my part when I don't see that promise through to the end.

It should be noted that "Duro" has continued to walk by my class *(he's already failing his new English class and the theatrics have begun anew)* and linger by the door like a lost puppy that couldn't wait to bolt the fence and then remembered the *food* was on *this* side.

The students have noticed, and asked me how I felt about that. I tell them I feel like we should be focused on what we're doing inside OUR classroom instead of who is outside of it.

A bit of a cop-out I'll admit, but it gets us back on task and gets me back to what I am paid to do:

Teach your kids *with* you, **not raise them *for* you.**

There we go.

Threshold Crossed.

No turning back now, which is good, because I'm starting to *like* this.

PART V
BELLY OF THE WHALE

The "Belly of the Whale" (so named from the mythical story of Jonah) is the metaphorical separation from the hero's known world and self. By entering this stage, the person shows their willingness to undergo some sort of metamorphosis; in short, they're "in it to win it" now.

I was angry again, and it felt good. Too many of my brothers and sisters in the education field were having their knees taken out from underneath them by everyone from passive-aggressive parents to fat, witch-hunting politicians.

I was determined, if nothing else, to expose some of the insidious crap that we feel the sting of every day, but of which the general public is blissfully ignorant.

Feelings were sure to be hurt, and my job security might suddenly become threatened. Don't care. I speak nothing but the truth and, as I said, I was angry again and, unlike Dr. Bruce Banner, you probably *will* like me when I'm angry.

Soundtrack for this chapter: *The Pot*—Tool.

Fifty Is the New Zero
(But You Wouldn't Know It.)

Obviously, the title for this chapter is a play on all these nonsense "re-thinkings" on fashion (brown is the new black,) aging (60 is the new 40,) and entertainment (*The Walking Dead* is the new *Teletubbies*.)

OK, I made that last one up, but you know what I mean.

What you may NOT know is that the idea for the title came from a "district directive" that my school initiated regarding our students (and that *many* schools practice *without the knowledge of many of the parents **of** those children.*)

Simply put, the educational staff received an Email from our curriculum and instruction czar informing us that <u>ALL failing grades, including zeros for completely ignoring an assignment, would be rounded up to a 61</u> (for 1st to 8th graders) <u>or a 50</u> (for 9th to 12th graders.)

I'll wait a minute while you process this,

and perhaps check and see if *your* school district engages in similar shenanigans?

As you might expect, I was not at all happy with this "district directive." I can't call it a **policy** because, a few weeks after it was put into place, a few parents found out (they were never formally told) and inquired about it at a School Board meeting. The Board's response went something like this:

"Huh? What are you talking about?"

Needless to say, the architects of this monument to low expectations started running from this policy faster than Usain Bolt at the Olympics. An Email was sent (Heaven forbid we do *anything* in person) informing us that the "half for nothing policy"—as the teachers came to call it—was, in fact, "not a policy but a *district directive.*"

TRANSLATION: "We're doing it anyway; even if the parents don't know about it and the board doesn't understand it." (Insert mustache twirling and sinister, super villain laugh.)

Did any of you out there read *Animal Farm* in high school? Do you remember how the pigs started using euphemisms and fancy language to abuse their power and further their exploitation of the other animals?

Yeah, something like that.

As you might expect, I was physically nauseous at the idea of rewarding the kid who blatantly ignored his Summer reading assignment with a *50*, while giving the kid next to him (who put in 200+ hours of reading, analyzing, and journal writing) a critical but fair *83*.

I guess I could have just given all of the kids that actually DID the assignment a high grade *(thereby falsifying every promise I made to them about keeping my standards high,)* or I could have looked for ways to "get those points back" from the slackers by "creatively grading" some of their future assignments *(thereby compromising the integrity I promised myself I would maintain,)* or I could have simply accepted that "rules are rules," and made my life easier by doing so. *(HaHAhAhaHa…yeah, THAT'll happen.)*

I know people that did all of the above, and I don't blame them for doing whatever they had to do to keep their jobs, but I think it is unconscionable that we were ever put in that position. Personally, I subscribe to the Yiddish Proverb that "stupidities that succeed are still stupidities."

Mr. Giant Zigadenus, our "district directive" czar, sent everybody the "F = 61 or 50" Email which, I kid you not, ended with the message that "it [was] important to set a clear precedent that reading during the summer [was] essential…"

Needless to say, anybody with even a passing interest in the quality of their students' education was appalled and offended. I thought maybe I would speak on behalf of our collective displeasure to the Superintendent but **Nobody Gets In To See The Wizard Not Nobody, Not No How**, so I sent an Email to Mr. Zigadenus, (speaking only on my behalf so as not to implicate any of my peers,) expressing my concern.

Mr. Zigadenus,

*I can only speak for myself, but I fail to see how rewarding 50 points to students who did absolutely nothing "set[s] a clear precedent that reading during the summer is essential and…a requirement." I find it grossly unfair to the students who complied with the summer reading requirements, **as did the negligent students themselves,** MOST of whom WANT the "0" they deserve, as they are cognizant that high standards = love, and that the soft bigotry of low expectations is already prevalent enough in their lives. My greater concern, of course, is why some students chose not to read at all, and I consider it my duty to rectify whatever was broken within them that made them stop loving reading, fully aware that it may be an excruciatingly long and individualized process. As per the grading system, I take great pride in holding my students to very high standards, and in cultivating a classroom environment where my students are strong enough to withstand the reality of accountability, and that approach has yielded students that excel in* *areas both externally quantifiable and internally empowering. Many of our student population already feel patronized knowing that a **58** (which rounds to a 60) is a passing grade here; when they become aware that complete failure gets you within 8 points of that mark, I fear we will have seriously dampened the fire to which Plutarch so eloquently referred. Dangerous, considering the hyper-competitive global economy into which we are sending them…*

Thank you for your time,

—Step

In the interest of complete honesty, there was some other *"I'm a good soldier, like all my brothers and sisters in the English Dept., so I'll play ball but the idea still sucks"* stuff at the end but I think you get the point.

Unfortunately, I had to wait almost a full work week for a reply; apparently, Mr. Zigadenus lacked the ability to send a simple "Hey Frank, thanks for your honesty, let's get together and talk about this" Email. After an uncomfortable amount of time, I received an extensive, very erudite, disgustingly politically correct response that did three things:

One, <u>Applauded</u> my "passion and interest in motivating students" while letting me know, oh so subtly, that the *"districtdirectivepolicy-whateverthehellyouwanttocallit"* was staying put.

Two, <u>Implied</u> that perhaps I was *lying* about my students WANTING zeros for undone work (**I wasn't, they did, and they did because even the dullest among them know that, as I told Giant in the letter, accountability = love.**)

Three, <u>Failed</u> to acknowledge that I might, just might, as a teacher, *TRY TO FIND OUT **WHY** A STUDENT DID NOT DO AN ASSIGNMENT, AND THEN **WORK WITH HIM** TO RECTIFY THAT SITUATION.*

I was hotter than Hell; I don't think it would be a stretch to say that the only reason Mr. Zigadenus still has all of his vertebrae is thanks to hours of anger management and shock therapy.

Thanks, Mom.

But if you think *I* was mad, you should hear what the *parents* of the students thought abou....

Oh, wait; silly me. I forgot.

*Most of them **didn't know.***

And the ones that should have been most aware of this couldn't even figure it out on their own *because they didn't have access to Revelations, the online grading system for the school.*

That's correct. Most of the PARENTS of the children (and read this carefully now) were unable to access their children's grades/comments/etc. via our *shiny new computer system*, largely because of ineptitude in getting access codes (via Emails and phone calls) *to* those parents *over the 2+ months* spent getting it "up and running." So... the Superintendent, the Director of Curriculum and Instruction, the Principal and Vice principals, the School Board, et.al could not, for some reason, combine their wonder powers and convey this new system to the parental units of the district? Interesting.

We, as teachers, are expected to stay in contact with the guardians of our kids and keep them updated no matter what.

The people making those demands?

Not so much.

--------------------**7 months later**----------------------

About HALF of the parents *still* don't have access to the computer system that now contains three report cards, three progress reports, and several thousand comments.

Interesting, because the 3 schools that *my children* go to have the same *Revelations* computer system, and we were hounded via Email, text and phone like we owed the government money until we accessed the system for each child and verified as such by Email.

Long story short—it can be done. If you **care.**

Even more interesting, most of the parents that fought through the fog of obscurity to GET access to their kids' grades were—you guessed it—the parents of the kids whose grades were pretty good.

Here we go again…involved parents, the ones that stay on top of their kids, tend to have the kids that don't *require* such oversight. But those parents will continue to stay involved and inquisitive and, dare I say, intrusive(?) until they have raised an ADULT that doesn't require supervision.

If you are one of those parents—
may whatever God you worship bless the living daylights out of you.

Meanwhile, there are two *other* groups of parents/guardians.*
*As with anything, these are by no means absolutes, but they are general trends that anybody working with kids will validate.

Some parents genuinely WANT to help their children, but for any number of reasons, need assistance to facilitate their involvement.

Some parents simply don't care.

These two animals could not be more different, but they share one unfortunate similarity: their kids usually have the kind of grades and behavior that need to be checked…often.

Then I gots ta thinkin'…

Maybe the powers-that-be,

the ones that continually ignore questions about the "half credit for no effort'" policy,

the ones that **preach** high expectations but **practice** uniformity,

don't WANT certain parents checking in, because they might, just might,

start asking questions.

Questions like: *"It says here in the 'comments' section that Martin didn't turn in ANYthing, even after he was given an extra day to do it, for this project, yet he received a 50 out of 100. I don't understand… shouldn't that be a zero?"*

or

"How come Andrew is allowed to play [insert sport] when his coach and teacher tells me he's failing [insert class(es)] and missing assignments? And why are there no zeros for assignments on his report card?"

We wouldn't want concerned, informed parents **asking questions** now would we?

Apparently not, especially when the people at the top of the food chain are cooking the books to make their "win percentage" look good. But hey, what's a little false advertising among friends? It's not like our *product* is the *future of this country* or anything.

Please keep two things in mind as you process this flying monkey circus of ridiculousness: One, this is all 100% true, and may be taking place in a school district near you. Two, THIS is the kind of crap that keeps *good* teachers from setting high standards for your kids that we truly *want* to enforce, but can't (without "breaking the rules.")

So the next time you ask your child's teacher why your kid:

- is passing a class that they shouldn't be passing without having adequately mastered the source material
- is allowed to play a sport, etc. for which they should be ineligible
- is growing up with a falsely inflated sense of their own ability but no sense of accountability whatsoever…

don't be surprised when we just take our finger and point to an imaginary spot above us on the educational "food chain."

And don't be surprised, especially if it's me, if I use a *particular* finger to do it.

PART VI
THE ROAD OF TRIALS

The road of trials is a series of tests, tasks, or challenges that the hero simply must undergo (and overcome) to begin the transformation. Often, the person faced with the trials will fail one or more (but still evolve from surviving the experience.)

Let me start with an apology. I am sorry for all of the things I left out here, but if I dedicated just *one page* to every trial the modern teacher faces, this book would have turned into something dwarfing the Harry Potter series pretty quickly.

There were a few monstrous adversaries that HAD to be addressed:

- **The parents** of our students, (who seem to be left out of every discussion of "what's wrong with kids these days?")
- The way **the system itself** (which seems determined to turn our children into test-taking automatons,) treats the aforementioned students.

In between THAT two-headed monster (and isn't that challenge enough?) I followed the sage advice to "go with what you know" and included **some of my own personal "trials"** which, I am sure, will sound an awful lot like some of yours.

Soundtrack for these sections/chapters:
So many possibilities, but let's go with:
(PARENTS) *Parents Just Don't Understand* by DJ Jazzy Jeff and the Fresh Prince
(MY OWN PRIVATE VAULT) *The Idiots Are Taking Over* by NOFX, **and**
(ANTI-TEACHER AMERICA) *Everything is Broken* by Bob Dylan.

SECTION 1
PARENTS: The Variable Nobody Wants to Talk About

"The roots run deep though my own backyard
The fruit goes bad and it don't fall far
Nothing good grows from a bad seed
You can find me hanging from the family tree."

—John Eddie *The Family Tree*

Listen, I'll keep this simple. If you're a parent, *your* involvement in your child's education is, perhaps, the single most important factor in determining their success in school. I have over a quarter century of experience teaching every age, ability level and social demographic. Couple that with thousands of hours of conversations [with other educators,] and I would be hard-pressed to say that there is any more accurate indicator of how well a student will do than the answer to the simple question:

"How involved is the parent?"

Of course, the *type* of involvement is critical.

I could refer you to about 100 different articles/studies on how over-protective, hyper-enabling parenting damages kids and turns them into fragile adults with no sense of accountability and (surprise, surprise) difficulty finding employment.

Conversely, there is an entire generation of students coming to us with virtually no parental guidance whatsoever. While I respect the effort these kids put forth trying to get through school with no frame of reference for how to handle basic social encounters, let alone constructive criticism, that doesn't change the fact that failing to give your kid a basic idea of what responsible, civil behavior looks like is unconscionable (and make a teacher's job near impossible.)

I see and hear statistics, studies, charts and chatter every day detailing the factors that determine the success (or, more appropriately of late, the reason for the failure) of our students. Apparently, everything from a proper breakfast to the rotational orbit of the planets is worthy of millions of [your tax] dollars of research, but nobody wants to bring up the fact that: **Some of the people who *conceived* the students might not be providing the greatest *role models* for the students.**

Trust me when I tell you I had to revise that last line about 1,000 times to make it *that* nice, especially considering some of the…interactions…I've had with the people posing as concerned parents. Of course, I am well aware that just about every teacher reading this book can probably top my stories, (we ALL, from kindergarten to graduate school, fight this fight;) however, that doesn't make my stories any less fun to read.

But that's a tease, isn't it?

Allow me to elaborate…

I'll c Wht I can do 4 U.

The tag line for the 1960s TV series *Naked City* claimed "there are eight million stories in the city." There are easily as many polluting the hallowed halls of education. Very often, they are enough to boil the blood of even the most cynical among you and, very often, they involve a veritable rogues gallery of clueless adults whose input (or lack thereof) has resulted in a less than stellar student product. Here is one of those stories, which I experienced firsthand. This should provide the uninitiated with a small glimpse into what we teachers deal with every day.

This year, I was assigned to teach 9th and 11th grade students. Someone in the brain trust decided that teachers shouldn't have students back to back, so you either taught 9/11 or 10/12. Even though that first pair of number is synonymous with disaster to most Americans, they both qualify in terms of the thought process behind them. I would LOVE to follow a class from freshman to senior year, and I know an awful lot of elementary teachers that would love to follow a class from 1st to 8th grades, *as is the practice in certain school systems that outperform us in every way.* (More on this later.)

Aaaaaaaanyway, I was teaching 9th and 11th grades this year, and one of the young men assigned to one of my 11th grade classes was Jabberwocky Loomis. Jabberwocky was, like a painful amount of students in our educational system: a walking, rarely talking example of what happens when the soft bigotry of low expectations meets parental enabling. Having been pushed ahead for God knows how many years, largely because nobody wanted to deal with him

AND because dad didn't:

"think he belong[ed] in one of them alternative programs... he don't need all that

extra stuff...y'all just ain't teaching him right...and he needs to be allowed to play

football 'cause he needs some motivation to study and all."

Right. So Jabberwocky winds up in my 11th grade COLLEGE PREPARATORY English Class (because we're *all* apples now!) and, as has happened so many times before, the resistant force runs into the immovable object, the part of which will be played by yours truly.

NOTE: Therein lies part of the problem, folks; Young Mr. Loomis has, sadly, and to his detriment, been handled with kid gloves his whole life.

I don't wear gloves.

In fact, you might say the only thing I wear to work on a regular basis are a matching set of brass knuckles called harsh reality and high expectations…and maybe a nice tie.

Jabberwocky Loomis got a 31 in my class for the first marking period, which was then promptly rounded up to a 50, (because the kid that has been written up for threatening staff and telling female teachers to suck his _____ is too sensitive to handle failure.) He followed this stellar performance by earning a ZERO for the first three weeks of the 2nd marking period, and it is at this point that we take up our story…

I had several "big boy" talks with Jabberwocky, where I treated him like a man and spoke directly to him about my expectations, his production, and the inevitable outcome, should he not change his ways *immediately.*

He tried to talk over me (didn't work,) he tried to deny everything (didn't work,) he tried to make every excuse under the sun (didn't work,) and he finished with the ever popular "whatever," which is the universal response for people not smart enough to verbalize their true emotions. (Didn't work.)

Sorry, but there was no way I was going to sit idle while this kid continued to, by virtue of standing still, move backwards socially and academically.

So I tried going through the counseling department. They understood "my frustration, but [couldn't] do anything without dad's permission, and [he] didn't think Jabberwocky needed to be in a more restrictive environment "'cause nothing [was] wrong with him."

NOTE: Therein lies part of the problem, folks; nobody ever SAID something was *wrong* with him. People that are *trained to recognize* social and learning issues *identified a need and offered to accommodate it.* EVERY individual learns differently, and some learners need an education outside the standard classroom setting, there is no shame in that; **however, the parent, for some reason** (guilt, perhaps?) **interprets this as some sort of indictment of his parenting skills, and** (in a moment of supreme selfishness) **refuses any assistance the child might need and attacks any person offering constructive criticism *about* the child.**

So I contacted the football coach, because Jabberwocky's dad was "concerned that this 'problem' could ruin his chances of playing." I, on the other hand, wanted to know why the heck this kid, who was failing every subject except gym, and had a list of discipline referrals longer than my leg, was even allowed to try out for the team. The football coach, not the sharpest saw in the tool shed himself, said that "[Loomis] probably wouldn't make the team."

NOTE: Therein lies part of the problem, folks; I didn't ASK if he was good enough to make the team, I asked WHY a student that was failing everything in life from social skills to academics was allowed the *privilege* of playing sports. (And don't give me your "the kid needs something" bull crap because, ironically, you're right—he needs adults that care enough to hold him accountable for...well, ANYthing.)

So I finally tracked down dad and called him until I got an answer. Dad was shocked, despite having read and signed several years of interim reports, report cards, failure notices, Summer school approvals and meeting requests (like the one from the week prior that he didn't show for) that Jabberwocky was in such dire academic straits, and wanted to know *"if I could just put together all of the work he owed me and the instructions and all so he could make it up."*

NOTE: Therein lies part of the problem, folks; it's not my JOB to *"put together all of the work" a student* owes me AGAIN, along with instructions and dates AGAIN. It's the STUDENT'S job to do it the <u>first time</u>, *like all the other students in the class manage to do.*

But I did. I printed out everything Jabberwocky owed me, (using my own printer to expedite the process) and wrote *detailed* instructions for each assignment, along with due dates that were highlighted, and placed them, in chronological order, in a folder, which I placed in a sealed manila envelope; never let it be said that I wasn't compassionate.

I then contacted dad and told him what I was sending home. He assured me that he would "get with [his son,] and the work would be done."

Any teacher reading this will tell you what's coming.

If you're *not* in the educational field, and you're burning up right now at the amount of effort I have expended on this walking liability and the amount of work I've done to compensate for the legion of spineless "adults" around him…

You ain't seen nothing yet.

I gave Jabberwocky Loomis the aforementioned sealed envelope, and told him that Poppa Loomis was expecting it. He grunted and took it.

You're *welcome*, punk.

Less than two hours later, a nice young man that I never actually had as a student (but who came to me periodically for help with his papers) excused himself for interrupting my class. He said that he "found this folder *on the floor*, **in the bathroom**, and [he] saw my name on some of the papers so [he] brought it to [me.]"

Yes, you read that correctly.

I'll give you a second to imagine how I felt at that moment. The students in my class, to their credit, put two and two together and remained quiet while I took a few deep breaths, made a phone call, sent a text, and resumed teaching.

Never let it be said that my students weren't compassionate.

Of course, the call and the text were directed to Mr. Loomis, basically informing him about what happened. I finished *both* with "you do what you feel you have to on your end, and I'll do what I have to do here."

This is the text I received—18 hours later—<u>exactly</u> as it was written:

I no, I got the voicemail & txt…(real name of his child) left it the batroom on an accident…He said he went 2 ur class later on when realized it was lost, but he said u had left already…he does not want 2 jeopardize playin ball and said it wuz not intentional…Thanks 4 letting me no Wht was going on…Please keep me informed if there is no change!!!!!…

I should probably point out that the name of his child was, I kid you not, *misspelled* in the text, but that would probably be piling on; at any rate, here was my immediate response:

No, sir, I don't believe it was an accident. First of all, the sealed envelope (which I told him you were expecting unopened) was torn open; secondly, I was in the building all day and (name of student, spelled correctly) knows EXACTLY where I am if he wanted to find me. I have extended more than a fair amount of courtesy to (name of student,) who responded by leaving work that I compiled for him on a bathroom floor; and, let's be honest Mr. ____, anybody with a zero in a class shouldn't make those kinds of "accidents." His packet is on the desk of his vice principal, who happened to be there when the student delivered it to me. (Name of student) can pick it up today, but if he misses one more assignment, and doesn't make up this work on time, then he will have made it clear that he doesn't care about the class, and will be graded accordingly.

I thought I showed remarkable restraint, but I'll leave that up to you, gentle reader. Of course, I received another grammatically adventurous response:

Ok....well, he said it was a mistake., so we will c Wht will happen as of now..Ill take 2 him & I'll C Wht I can do 4 U. Thank u and have a blessed day!!

I always love the "have a blessed day" part, particularly when you know the parent wants to cut your head off and stick it on a pike for the unforgivable sin of pointing out how their over enabling ways and low expectations have created an 18 year-old chronic liar with a sense of entitlement and the reading level of my 8 year-old niece.

Wait, that's an insult—my 8 year-old niece could read circles around him.

Before I go any further, let me ask all of you teachers out there: Show of hands, how many of you could insert a student of your own into the (name) section and have this be dead-on accurate?

I'll bet there are a lot of hands across America.

Now, how many of you think I was being unfair, unprofessional, non-compassionate, racist, and/or a poopy head for being so mean to poor Jabberwocky and his dear ol' dad?

Well, you are certainly entitled to your opinion; and you would not be alone. I was accused of all of the above, in one form or another, when these events became public knowledge. The truly heartwarming part is that some of those accusations were hurled by some of my teaching "colleagues;" most of whom accuse the rain of being unfair, unprofessional, non-compassionate, racist, and poopy headed for getting them wet.

I'm sure they're probably right but—just in case—let's fast forward and see what happened with our punished protagonist and his improperly punctuating matriarch.

In the meantime, you have a blessed day.

...I waited exactly 5 weeks, and I have two confessions to make.

The first thing I'd like to confess is that I had an ending to this chapter already written; I figured (after all of my similar experiences) that I knew *exactly* how this would end. I would just have to fill in dates and times and a few proper nouns and Bang! Chapter finished.

But Jabberwocky Loomis defied the odds for a while. He started coming to class (almost always on time!) doing most of his assignments, and behaving reasonably well. Dad, the vice principal, and JL were all thrilled. His guidance counselor was positively over the moon, and expressed his sanctimonious joy to me.

"Yeah...that's great," I snarled, "What, exactly, are your qualifications for this job, Mr. Loomis? Well, I show up on time a lot, do most of my work, and behave if everything is going my way and I get twenty chances to fix my mistakes...he'll be employed in **no** time."

Guidance counselors don't usually like me.

Now, I didn't say that he *did* much when he was in class, that the work was *quality* work, or that he was *productive*, only well-behaved...for a while.

So the verbatim prognostication I had typed and saved had to be deleted, 'tis true, but the chips still fell the way I thought they would, albeit just not in the time frame I expected. I may not have covered the point spread, but I got the winner of the game right.

But you said, not two paragraphs ago, that Jabberwocky surprised you and got it [kinda] together.

Yes, I did; I said that Jabberwocky Loomis did, indeed, defy the odds *for a while.*

After two weeks of trying desperately to behave, produce, and learn like a somewhat below average citizen student, JL's teachers, tutors and coach (of course, he got a shot at the football team; after all, he hadn't killed anyone and he could sign his name) the pressure got to be too much, and he went off the rails. He started getting discipline referrals in bunches, cutting classes, and generally letting anyone that wasn't deaf, dumb, and blind know that he didn't want any part of the "real world" of school.

Dad, the vice principal and the guidance counselor didn't know what the heck was going on.

"How could this happen?" "He was doing so well!" "Doesn't he like school?" and my personal favorite, *"What are these teachers doing to make him behave like this?"*

It should be noted that I was in contact with Poppa Loomis almost every day via extremely long, detailed texts about Jabberwocky's performance in my class.

I figure after about week one he seriously regretted finally asking, after 11 years of his son failing classes and being moved from schools, for someone to "keep him posted so he could get him in line."

I figure after week four he was secretly happy that his little enablement experiment folded like origami just so he wouldn't have to hear from me ever again. Strangely, I wasn't on the list of teachers he blamed for his son's 127th fall from grace.

TEACHING TIP from your ol' Uncle Step—if a parent that is clearly negligent and enabling tries that "just keep me posted and I'll straighten his a right out" stuff, do what I do—hit them with an iceberg of information big enough to sink their Titanic game of "let's pretend" and *keep it up*. It's exhausting, but: A) it establishes *anus***

protectus **from a legal perspective, and B) it's soooo worth it when the inevitable happens.**

And the inevitable sounds like *"How could this happen?" "He was doing so well!" "Doesn't he like school?"* and *"What are these teachers doing to make him behave like this?"*

Then they asked my opinion.

I won't tell you exactly what I said, but I'll bet you can guess.

None of them liked it,

but none of them argued it,

because ALL of them shared the blame.

I felt a little bad as I left that meeting but, as the Assyrian proverb says: *If the thunder is not loud, the peasant forgets to cross himself.*

Jabberwocky Aspertame Loomis was officially transferred to an "alternative school placement" (bad kid program) where he would receive "a curriculum in keeping with his special educational and social needs" (just enough supervision and worksheets to qualify as public education) so that he "might eventually realize his academic promise" (get a diploma that isn't worth the paper it's printed on so he can leave it in a drawer and go be a barber *which he's been saying from 7th grade he wanted to do.)* Last I heard, he came almost every day, put his head down, and proceeded to (during his wakeful hours) make himself a hemorrhoid for any and all attempting to educate him. I have had more than one teacher from the program remark that "now [they] know why even I couldn't take this [kid.]"

I have to confess,

I was sad.

Profoundly, personally, and professionally sad.

Sad the way only somebody who tries—in a few months, to fix **years** of inadequate adults, dangerous peers and questionable role models—feels.

No, I feel no sense of "I told you so."

Yes, I feel some sense of responsibility.

No, I don't expect it to change, but I'll keep trying to change it, because that's my job. So keep sending me your damaged, disenfranchised kids that haven't been listened to, loved or treated like anything but objects to collect an SSI check or produce testing data, then wonder, in amazement, *why* they go bad.

Meanwhile, I'll c Wht I can do 4 U.

Even the Involved Parents Get It Wrong Sometimes.

OK, before we get started let me make one thing crystal clear: I'll take the "over-involved" parent over the deadbeat, "he-don't-act-like-that-at-home" parent 93 out of 100 times. Of course, there are those times when even well-intentioned parental support becomes a wee bit overzealous and, dare I say, *enabling*.

Ssshhhh...hear that? That's the sound of thousands of teachers shaking their heads in affirmation.

I deal predominately with one parent (if that) households where the phone number often changes week to week (and is sometimes NOT within the area code of the school district,) so I have limited contact with parental units that think, by virtue of their annual gross, that *they can tell me how to do my job.* But I've been doing this for a long time, so I have, on occasion, encountered this rare beastie. Usually, I remind them, not so subtly, that "they spent 15-16 years building the house before I moved in for a few hours a week, so if the foundation is shaky..."

They don't like that, at all.

I don't care.

Those meetings ALWAYS end with me politely reminding them that they are, after all, *in charge* (they love that,) so "feel free to have your child transferred out of my class."

Funny, they never seem to want to do that.

Good parents are very primitive in their love of their kids, and they can *smell* threats and assets to their children, and I (for the most part) am certainly the latter...at least the *first* three letters.

Now when this little anecdote went down, I confess to being surprised. I had been told, several weeks into the school year, that a new student, Bozworth Botulism, would be showing up in my class. (This happens with frightening frequency all year long, trust me.) Of course, it would be on *me* to get up to speed about his profile, previous grades, special needs (if any,) writing folder, etc. etc. etc. etc. because the people that switch kids around like dispensable pawns in chess don't concern themselves with such pedestrian tasks.

Oh, and by the way, he's starting tomorrow.

Lovely.

To compound the joy, I was informed that his parents were "very involved" (intrusive,) wanted Bozworth in a "gifted" class (already pissed about his placement and ready to spew venom,) and were a bit upset about how the whole placement process worked (the aforementioned venom will be aimed at YOU, Mr. Step, because the people that facilitate such classroom placements don't concern themselves with such pedestrian tasks.)

I love it.

Actually, in almost all cases like this, once I get ahold of the kid and we start working together, all misplaced anxiety and righteous rage dissipates and we can get down, pretty quickly, to the business of readin' and writin'. In this manner, I understand that I differ tremendously from some of my teaching brethren, who are *continually* browbeaten by overzealous offspring management systems.

Sadly, even if you think you've hit the "educator employment lottery" and wind up teaching in the district where every kid has an iPad, internet, two parents and books at home, be careful...

Sometimes that means you gotta deal with Ms. Lawyer, Daddy Dentist, and their white collar sense of entitlement that leads to conversations that start with *"well, since I pay your salary..."*

But I digress...

Back to Bozworth and his debut in my class.

Nice kid, very polite, definitely a cut above the mixed bag of academic mutts that so often make up an incoming freshman class, but not so much as to make me run like my head was on fire to the counseling department screaming "for the love of God save this kid and get him into a gifted class NOW ere another precious, exceptional brain cell be compromised!"

NOTE: Don't laugh, I said those exact words about a student several years ago and damn if she didn't get moved to a gifted class the following week; she is currently studying biological engineering at "Prominent" University.

But I digress...again.

Mr. Botulism was a good student, a good kid, and he was going to have a good year if he kept his nose clean and *asserted himself.*

And "therein lies the rub." (Big Willy Shakespeare, *Hamlet*)

Most "smart kids," for a variety of reasons (*Cough cough....lazy English teachers who reward* **quantity** *of writing with good grades without taking time to critique the* **quality**...*cough*) learned, during their time in school that long, neatly written answers often = good grades, even if the kid was talking about *Tom and Jerry* when he should have been analyzing *Of Mice and Men.*)

The aforementioned teachers, and you **almost** can't blame them, are so happy to have a nice kid who actually does his homework and puts some effort into the projects, that they reward them with grades that might stroke the little bugger's ego and (here is where it gets sticky) dilate their sense of just how well-educated they really are. Inevitably, little Alvin, Simone and Theodora ascend through the ranks of elementary, middle and intermediate school with bright smiles, perfect attendance awards, and (well deserved, don't get me wrong) academic certificates that, while nice, inflate their sense of how smart they really are, filling their little entitlement balloons with hot air, until they drift too close to a very sharp object, often lodged somewhere in a crevice atop Mount High Expectation.

Sometimes, that sharp object looks a lot like me.

Anybody else out there see a sharp object when they look in the mirror? Then you've probably enjoyed a bit of dialogue like the one that follows. Please understand, I take no pleasure whatsoever in bursting the metaphorical bubble surrounding these [somewhat] sheltered kids; in fact, I get a little tired of being the first door that doesn't automatically swing open just because they stepped in front of it.

Bozworth Botulism arrived in class as we were finishing *The Hunger Games*. I figured (since everyone on the home front swore he was "gifted" material) that he would be able to

knock out the parts of the book he missed in the two weeks prior to the final test.

NOTE: I taught a class of so-called "gifted and talented" students for three years *(even a blind squirrel finds a nut once in a while)* and what I was asking Boz to do was almost embarrassingly easy by 'GT' standards.

In the meantime, we were going to be reading *The Handmaid's Tale*, another dystopian novel with a similar theme, which Bozworth had already read (as it was on the gifted class Summer reading list, and he assumed he would be in a gifted class.) No harm, no foul, no worries. Boz would still learn a *lot* of things about *Handmaid's Tale* and dystopian literature in general, and I would give him another similar novel to read independently (that he and I would work on separately) so he wouldn't be bored or academically stagnant.

Extra work for me, but worth it if the kid is engaged and into it.

I gave him a copy of Orwell's classic *1984* and told him everything I just told you, albeit in more detail and face to face; Boz accepted the book and seemed to welcome the individual attention and responsibility.

Or so I thought.

MISter Botulism, an obviously well-meaning patriarch (and, to be honest, one of the few involved biological DADS that I had the pleasure of encountering in recent memory,) contacted me with his concerns.

It should be noted that Bozworth himself never voiced *two words* of concern to me; alas, another frequent side effect of being one of the "smart kids" is that you tend to be fragile, as in parents-fight-your-battles-for-you fragile.

You can just visualize the Boz balloon drifting dangerously close…

Guess what? Sometimes parents need a little air taken out of their balloons too.

I received the following Email (which I have grammatically corrected/changed a bit for legal reasons but kept the original intent/flavor) two days after I gave Boz the copy of *1984*.

Dear Mr. Stepnowski,

I am a little confused about the assignment that you gave Bozworth. I understand that he already read The Handmaid's Tale over the summer since I thought that he was being placed in GT, but since he switched into your class in December he did not read Hunger Games in its entirety. He only read the last 2 chapters that you were doing in class. The assignment that you want him to do is to compare Hunger Games to 1984. In order to do this he will have to read 2 books independently, won't he?!? I feel that he is now being punished for the extra work that he did over the summer rather than getting credit for it since you are requiring him to do extra independent work that the rest of the class is not doing. Shouldn't he be reading Hunger Games and doing the same essay as the rest of the class? Believe me, my son is not afraid of work. I am just frustrated with the way this whole scheduling disaster has been handled. I do not feel that any of you have been considering my son in any of their decisions. If you could please

(and this is where my "sharp edges" emerged)

explain your reasoning then I may be able to explain it to Bozworth. Thank you. — Mr. Botulism

Just in case you weren't counting—that's 7 uses of the pronoun "I" in a short paragraph that is, allegedly, about *the kid*. You weren't counting?

I was.

And with that I sent my immediate response, which has been presented, for your enjoyment, in its pristine state.

Dear Mr. Botulism,

Thank for contacting me with your concerns. Please allow me to get two things out of the way before I explain my reasoning to you. First and foremost, please don't lump me in with whomever has been "making decisions about him" up until this point; I wasn't involved in any of the process that culminated with Bozworth in my class, and I have done nothing but teach him to the best of my ability (talking great pains to ensure that he stays challenged) since that time. Secondly, I think we can both agree that, at his age, you shouldn't **have** *to "explain [my] reasoning to Bozworth." He should have come to me with his concern, and I would have gladly rectified the issue— as I did today when he and I spoke. If Boz is legitimately worthy of being in a Gifted class (and he does show signs of that, academically) then he should also manifest the social maturity necessary—in this case, speaking up for himself—to be in a class of that type as well. Maybe he had bad experiences with prior teachers in doing so(?) Again, I'm not them and I expect the same benefit of the doubt I extend to my students.*

After speaking to Bozworth today, he seems comfortable with approaching me with any future issues, and he will, in fact, be reading the Hunger Games and consorting with me about it, as opposed to reading 1984. Bozworth gave me the impression that he HAD read

Hunger Games in its entirety (and the quality of his responses regarding the novel certainly validated

that,) so my intent was simply to keep him challenged, as it was made clear to me (by everyone except Boz himself, of course) that he already read The Handmaid's Tale.

*Bottom line: Bozworth Botulism learned three things today: to be proactive in his approach to classroom problems [at least in this class,] that his **reading** of The Handmaid's Tale is a far cry from my **teaching** of The Handmaid's Tale (as his last quiz grade certainly shows) and that his father and his teacher care enough about him to communicate quickly when he's concerned.*

I hope that clears up any confusion; I can always be reached with any further questions at this Email address. Thanks for your parental involvement in your child's education, THAT is becoming an all-too-rare delicacy in the daily buffet of a teacher.

Be well,
Mr. Step

Believe me, I almost signed it "You have a blessed day."

Never did hear back from Botulism Sr. (shocking, I know) but I *did* talk to Boz in person the next day and tried to explain to him, in a funny and casual way that "you need to speak up brother…I'm not going to bite you…just let me know when you've got a concern, ok?" He nodded like his head was going to dislodge, which worried me because any 15 year-old boy that can't make eye contact and speak audibly when a grown man is talking to him is the psychological equivalent of veal, and needs a bit of real world toughening up.

Sure enough, the next day when I asked him if he had any questions yet about *The Hunger Games,* he mumbled (trying to maintain eye contact but looking like it was *killing* him to do so) "You didn't give it to me yet. I returned my copy and I need one to read."

Times like this, I feel compelled

nay, **obligated**

to fast forward such brittle balloon boys into something vaguely resembling young adulthood.

"Boz," I said, coldly enough to lower the temperature in the room about 10 degrees, and lowering my face to his and swaying like a cobra to *force* him to maintain eye contact, "when, exactly, did you think you were going to tell me that? Or were you going to have dad shoot me another Email?"

Something faintly resembling pride shone for a second in Bozworth Botulism's eyes, and he locked eyes with me for a second.

Contrary to what you may think, I liked that, and I told him so.

"Now, for future reference, Botulism, YOU (and the cobra poked the balloon ever so lightly in his chest) will tell me anything involving YOU, whether it be good or bad, in this class. In fact, YOU can approach me about anything if you just want to talk, but YOU are the one getting the grade in this class, and *I* am the one giving it, so there need be no further variables in this equation. Are we *crystal* clear, Botulism?"

"Yes, Mr. Step."

A polite auditory response,

loud enough to be definitive,

with sustained eye contact—that's the trifecta of student evolution right there, folks!

Let that be a lesson to YOU, parents of "the smart kids."

Believe me, we (the teachers) love and respect you for being involved and sending your children to us ready to learn *and capable of doing so.*

You have *no idea* how much we thank you for that, especially in this age of apathy and non-accountability—

but we have a job to do, too, and sometimes that involved being the first teacher to ever say "no, this isn't good enough " to your child.

Sometimes, we need to be the wall that they have a hard time climbing, because they will have learned something about themselves in getting over us—and we will all be the better for it when your kid goes out into the world with the *confidence* to <u>implement</u> the intellect your diligence ensured would be there.

BOTTOM LINE: Your kids can handle the criticism that we, their teachers, must impart upon them in order to facilitate their evolution as students, so let them *fight for themselves*, that way their social skills can catch up to their classroom ability. Trust me; they'll need them both in equal measure.

Thus endeth the sermon, go in peace

Incivility, Racism, Ignorance, and Enablement.
The Four Horsemen of the Edupocalypse

Yes, they exist.

No, (despite what some people think) not one single race, religion, group or demographic has the market cornered on them.

And yes, sadly, these unholy ideals often arise in school; in fact, I'll go as far as to say that *the complicated business of educating children often **exacerbates** these issues*. I can only speak from my experiences, but I am a white male who, for more than half of my life, has taught, for the most part, teenagers of different races, religions, and [obviously] generations of mine.

That being said, I could have written an entire book about my clashes with "guardians" and "advocates" who wanted my head on platter, my license revoked, and formal apologies issued because I had the audacity to expect more from their kids than they did,

(and the crime of *looking* differently than "them" while doing it.)

NOTE: If I included similar stories from my teaching brothers and sisters across the country, I could have written a SERIES of books that would have rivaled George R.R. Martin in page count.

NOTE TO <u>SELF</u>: Seriously consider authoring *Game of Moans* series; option TV rights to HBO.

In the meantime, I'm still teaching, head intact, and I have *never* issued an apology to someone who *demanded* one.

Know why?

BECAUSE THE *KIDS* CAN HANDLE THE TRUTH; those of you who have read anything by me before knew that was coming because it is a recurring theme with me. <u>The students</u> (and, to be fair, the *involved, realistic* parents and protectors) <u>know that rigor requires effort; effort requires motivation, and *that* level of motivation can only be sustained by…dare I say it?</u>

<u>Love.</u>

That might be important, so I'll say it again, more crudely, albeit more simply.

If I'm pushing your kid to excel, that's because I love them enough to sustain the kind of effort (usually associated with *good **parenting***) to DO so.

Of course, the sad truth is still the truth, and the truth is that some people don't know how to handle the type of love that involves accountability because they've never been given the means to do so.

In fact, more and more of the students I teach are products of "guardians" who are clearly embarrassed of their [lack of] parenting and, rather than look for help, talk openly about their fears, or try to work *together*…

they attack us, the teachers, for trying harder to reach their kids than they did.

I completely understand the misplaced anxiety that comes from raising a child, and I have, on *many* occasions, lashed out (in a moment of exhaustion/frustration) at others for something I felt guilty about.

However, I never, EVER (in those situations) went after the people I was venting on in a personal manner. I never *accused them of having fundamental flaws in their character*, nor did I try to *ruin their livelihoods* or *damage them physically or emotionally*.

Sadly, pathetically, all the aforementioned have been done to me and my teaching brethren, and most of those incidents were fueled by bigotry, racism, ignorance and enablement.

Several years ago, I was told, flat out, by a mother that I couldn't "understand," hence, "properly teach" her daughter because she [the student] was a Hispanic girl. In my fantasy world, I could have teleported the thousands of young Hispanic and Latino women I've taught over the years into the room to offer what I will generously call "an opposing viewpoint." Instead, I asked her if she limited her business with doctors, dentists, accountants, landscapers, mechanics, clergymen, police, lovers and lawyers to people of her gender and ethnicity.

She didn't like that. She said it was (expletive) ridiculous.

I said that I agreed.

Sadly (and yes, I'm getting as tired of that word as you are) her daughter sat there, *mortified*, at having wrought this upon me when, in a moment of totally understandable weakness, she complained, tearfully, that the paper I was asking her to rewrite was "really hard." So I completely understood, and *respected* "mama bear" wanting to protect her cub; but the **child** made it clear that she wasn't angry at me, the **child** made it clear that any shortcomings were her own. The **child** made it clear that I had done everything under the sun to help her, et cetera et cetera until you want to puke…

But the **parent** felt the need to make it personal, the **counselor** (most of which I find to be invertebrate in nature) *facilitated* that by placating the mother's verbal accusations prior to my arrival, and a **vice principal** numbly questioned why I didn't *"just apologize, to [shut her up,] and move on with my life."*

The parent left, feeling (I guess) better about herself. (NOTE: when I explicitly asked her if she'd like her daughter removed from my class she said "no.") The counselor went on floating the way jellyfish do, and the vice principal has moved "up the ladder" the way people of his ilk tend to do in business.

The student apologized profusely to me the next day, and I to her, and she eventually completed a research paper that (according to a very recent Facebook message) *"helped [her] immeasurably manifest her evolution as a student;"* thereby impressing her professor with, what he called, her *"rare attention to detail and direction."*

Yep, clearly failed to connect with that one.

Maybe if I had been a Hispanic female…

Boy, if I had a nickel for every time I wished THAT.

All joking aside, I had my say about "the race card" in my first book; and ignorance is the stone I am forced , like Sisyphus, to roll up the hill every day only to watch it come back and crush me again. Unfortunate flaws in human character tend to explode exponentially when people's children are the "product" in question. Unfortunately, some folks—who happen to be shaping the citizenry of tomorrow— allow their fragile egos and preconceived notions to guide them when they [over]react to what they **perceive** to be educators "picking on" their kids.

They don't refer to aggressive acts of execution as "extreme prejudice" for nothing.

And hey, speaking of aggressive acts, at least the aforementioned mom didn't threaten to assault me; to call up *that* warm and fuzzy memory I have to go back a few years. *Mind you, as a teacher, I shouldn't have* **ANY** *memories of being physically threatened by parents, but I have* **several,** *as do—again—many of the teachers I know.*

Long story short, we had a student (let's call him Romeo for irony's sake) at my former place of employment that was gay.

Flamboyantly gay.

He was also braver than a cobra farmer who worked without a snake-bite kit.

Believe me when I tell you that walking the halls in a school comprised almost entirely of students with criminal records in a skirt, skin tight (pre-Underarmour) shirt and make up takes *significant* testicular fortitude. Nonetheless, Romeo was forced to fight his way through more than one verbal altercation/sexual harassment. (I shudder to think how many charges could have been leveled on Romeo's behalf with today's bullying laws.)

Romeo, unlike his literary counterpart could, in his words, "fight [his] sweet little ass off," but that didn't do him any good when he got surrounded by five of our school's finest; a veritable Hitler Youth of intolerance and violent bravado (as long as they were all together, of course.)

It just so happened that yours truly and a female computer teacher (let's call her Stephanie, because that was her name) rounded the corner just in time to intervene in what the head charmer, Brad Swaggart, affectionately called "piñata the faggot."

Those of you who have read my first book know that I was afforded a great deal of autonomy in my years working with [what were then called] "severely emotionally disturbed" youth. You also know that I react viscerally to bullies, so I had no problem firing off to Brad that "you know, psychiatrists say that the people most offended by homosexuality are, in fact, gay themselves."

Stephanie laughed. Romeo laughed. A few of the gestapo children themselves snickered. Mr. Swaggart did not. He, predictably, inquired—very loudly—(spittle flying from his mouth) "You callin' me a faggot?!"

"Noooooooo," I teased. "First of all, I don't *use* that word, because it's offensive, kind of like when people call you 'douchebag.' I mean, everyone knows you're not a product used for feminine..." at this point, Romeo's laughter and my increasing physical proximity to the "Aggravated Assault Club" made Brad, and a few of his cronies lose it. Insults were hurled, threats were made, posturing was done, and promises of revenge were uttered. I just stood there with that Mr. Blonde smile that asks *"Are you gonna bark all day little doggie, or are you gonna bite?"*

They left. Romeo thanked me, and I told him that "a nice pair of knee socks was a much better accompaniment to his plaid skirt than those silly things he was wearing." He laughed, reminded me that "Step, you craaaaaazy," said "bye bye" to Stephanie, and on he went.

The very next day,

and if I'm lyin' I'm dyin,'

I overheard a call on the walkie talkie of one of the behavior management team (think "school bouncers") saying—and I *still* can't believe this actually happened—that there were four guys at the gate and they say "they ain't leaving until they kick the faggot lover that insulted their son's ass."

You want to know how you KNOW you're a born English teacher?

You hear that broadcast and you instantly want to correct the improper grammar BEFORE you make your way to the gate...

Long story short.: Father of the year and three of his buddies were on the other side of the gate (with Brad) and the minute they caught sight of me began calling me a variety of terms that, were I of a more fragile nature, might have hurt me very deeply.

I tried, I really did. I asked Brad to please go to the truck while his father and I spoke. Dad and his cronies told him to stay, because they wanted him to see how "real men" behaved. I asked him if he was sure this was the type of behavior he wanted his son to emulate. The answer I received was unprintable.

It seems surreal (and, to be honest, deeply offensive) that being 6'4," 260+ lbs., and trained in multiple martial disciplines and firearms, etc. should matter when you're a TEACHER; however, the confidence that comes with that skill set has served me well on occasion.

This was one of them. I started climbing the fence.

My friends from the behavior management team stopped me (I knew they would) but the 4 bullies on the other side of the fence 'flinched' when I hit the fence (I knew they would) and Brad *saw* it (I knew he would.) I told Dad, and his BFFs that I was done at 2:10 and I would be leaving at that *exact* spot, alone, if he wanted to be there.

I did.

He wasn't (I knew he wouldn't.)

Oh, and I wasn't alone; cocky but not crazy, folks.

Not surprisingly, I eventually got around to talking to Brad and we developed a guarded, but legitimate dialogue that, I think

I hope,

opened his eyes a little to how "real men" really behaved, and bigotry and homophobia are nowhere on the list of behaviors.

I am proud to say that (and I had forgotten all about this until I started rewriting this story) Brad was one of the first kids to come up to me when I returned to school after the death of my son Cain. He seemed authentically upset and I think that showed an empathy that may have been missing there before. I certainly hope so, as I never heard from him after I left that particular place of employment.

VERY long shot, but if you're out there reading this, "Brad Swaggart"—you know who you are—go ahead, make my day (via Facebook or Twitter.)

These are but two isolated incidents in my own 25 years in the business. I'm just one man, and I have seen it in every conceivable combination: racial, socioeconomic, sexual, religious, you name it.

The following scenario plays out ***every day*** in the schools of America. TEACHERS—insert whatever 'differences' you choose to meet your own particular experiences, but I'll bet all of you have danced this dance:

1. I have been teaching the kid for less than a year (so that's probably, in terms of hours, less than 8 days TOTAL) and now…
2. I have asked him/her to push beyond their comfort level in my class because, as I said earlier, I CARE about them. (Oh, and by the way—I am now judged/graded/EMPLOYED based on their performance.) But unfortunately…
3. I don't **look, think,** or **act** the way the <u>parent</u> does, and that fact (which went "unnoticed" for several months,) somehow *now* makes me unfit to teach the kid.
4. Meanwhile, a veritable entourage of people (many of whom look, think, and act just like me) have been content to let the kid get pushed through the system even though they aren't *learning* a damn thing; but since they don't "bother"

the parent with minor details like *actual social* and *academic evolution*, they're just fine.

Got that?

Caring = more drama.

Apathy = under the radar.

Don't believe me?

Allow me to entertain you with one last story which, serendipitously, happened (I swear on the heads of my four children) *WHILE I WAS WRITING THIS BOOK*. I often joke with my comrades that sometimes my books "write themselves."

Never was this more the case.

I will stick to the facts, but **please understand that I have endured very similar incidents more times than I care to recount**, (and just about every teacher I know has as well.)

Ready?

William Sikes sat near the window in my 4th period class. William wasn't a bad kid [for me;] if anything, I found him to be painfully quiet, which is interesting for reasons that will become apparent later.

I gave an assignment near the end of the year which asked the students to choose one of four literary criticisms of a short story we read together. They had to read and annotate the criticism, then summarize it in 2-3 pages. (NOTE: I already walked the students through two identical assignments, this is their chance to prove that they can do this "on their own" going into 12th grade.)

NOTE: "On their own" is in quotes because to be honest, they have FIVE DAYS in class to work on their paper, submit it to me for revision, and edit their mistakes; basically, enough to time to ensure that they have a perfect paper by week's end. I even enlisted the help of another good (and very generous) teacher to come in during that period so we could get to everyone in real time. <u>Oh, and I gave them</u>

a sample first page so they could, literally, hold their paper next to my paper and check if _theirs_ looked (font, heading, margins, title, header, etc.) the same as _mine._

Yes, gentle reader; this is what passes for "College Prep" in some schools these days.

Bill Sikes turned in a paper that, in addition to having the _wrong font, wrong title_ and _wrong margins_ (?!?) also had the teensy problem of being _one hundred percent plagiarized._ When I pointed this out to Mr. Sikes, his answer was dumbfounding, and I've heard it _all._

"I didn't plagiarize."

"Uh…ok," I replied "Let's try this _again._ HERE is the original text, and HERE is your paper, you'll notice all the highlighted and numbered stuff? That's where you copied, word-for-word. Now…your excuse is?"

"You and (name of teacher helping me out) should have told me that and helped me."

"You know damn well what plagiarism is. Furthermore, you had a WEEK to turn in _anything_ and _everything;_ you submitted two handwritten paragraphs TOTAL and (teacher's name) _told_ you that your work sounded like it was right from the article."

"Why you pickin' on me?"

Needless to say, it didn't get any better from there. Three phone calls to step-mom's three different numbers and two lengthy Emails earned…

You guessed it. No response.

Contacting his counselor earned…

A soft "talking to" about "how you can't use other people's words" and a 2:00 meeting the next day with Bill's step-mother, who (thanks to Bill's lies and the counselor's fear of confrontation) was coming in, guns blazing, for my job and my head, in no particular order.

Thanks for nothing, and here we go again.

But first, let me tell you **what I was accused of, for _caring:_**

because I'm pissed off now,
because you need to know this,
because this is why so many teachers quit this job.

One, I was accused of singling out the student. Two, I was accused of "threatening to go back and change grades," and three, I was accused of picking on Bill. Of course, the obligatory racism accusation surfaced as well.

One: In 7 months, Billy the kid had managed to accrue 30 discipline referrals, including 3 in-school suspensions and one out of school suspension for cursing out a teacher, NONE of them came from me (but I'M singling him out?)

Two: Neither I, nor any teacher, has the access capability to go back in time and change report card grades that were already entered. (On a personal note, I think the intermediary could have addressed *that* issue with step-mom prior to the fireworks, but guidance counselor Danny Doormat's fear of confrontation prevented that.)

Three: *Picking* on him? Let me tell you a little about Billy the kid and YOU decide:

- Despite having been in *Summer School* (where he didn't impress anyone) *for failing English the previous year,* he was placed in a College Prep English class, MY College Prep class.
- First marking period interim report? 2 unsatisfactory ratings (out of 6 subjects.) 1st report card? 73 grade point average. *Right after the 1st report card I told step-mom, at parent-teacher conferences, that I would only contact her if something that would concern me as a parent happened; otherwise, we agreed, the monthly Emails and interims/report cards would be more than enough, and she could contact me with ANY questions/concerns.*
- Second marking period? 3 "unsatisfactory" ratings. 65 grade point average.

- Third marking period? 5 "unsatisfactory" ratings. 59 grade point average (and that "60" included a bunch of those "magic 50s" we talked about back in an earlier chapter; his real average was probably a LOT lower.
- Mid-Fourth marking period (the time of our "meeting?") Failing *almost every subject* badly…like *single digits* badly.

Oh, and the racism implication? Believe me when I tell you that I have become *numb* to that accusation because I've grown tired of intellectually clobbering the idiots who accuse me of it. I am not racist—these days, I think just about *everyone* sucks; and you're going to have to *earn* my respect no matter <u>who you are </u>or <u>where you come from</u>.

Two questions—Where was step-mom (self-professed "concerned parent") during this well documented downward spiral? and

Why weren't any other teachers (whose classes he was failing *worse than mine*) accused of the things of which I had been accused?

Don't know the answer to question #1 but I can tell you the answer to #2—because I was the only one that made the categorically stupid mistake of caring about whether or not her kid actually *learned* something. I actually made the ridiculously generous offer for him to take two days and rewrite the paper for partial credit. (NOTE: In most colleges, the *least* that would have happened was immediate failure of the course *for the year* and academic probation.)

Step-mom wanted to know why I was *only* giving him a few day days (to rewrite a paper that SHOULD have been done in class?!?) AND wanted to know—and this is a *direct quote*—

"What was the incentive to rewrite a paper if he was only going to get a [failing grade]?"—**IGNORANCE**

Oh…I don't know, how about actually learning something that you don't know and that could eventually cost you your college enrollment?

Continuing, step-mom wanted to know why I didn't call her. I told her that I sent her two long Emails. She replied

"Oh, I don't check my Emails, I'm busy; I (insert what she does at work.)"

I shot back, "And I'm not? I have 120 students and four kids of my own."

She repeated, loudly and dismissively, *"you should have called me."*

I smiled. "And you should check your Emails."

She didn't like that, no sir; but she was going to like it even less by the time I was done.

Step-mommy-dearest made an innocuous remark that "these teachers at (name of school) don't know 'bout these kids so they think they can just put they business out there." When I asked for clarification, I was given the impression that, unless we lived their lives, we couldn't relate to our students enough to "teach them right."
—INCIVILITY

"You know, I get that from a lot of the parents…"

She nodded, like she won something.

"of the kids that are *failing.*"

She stopped nodding. Fast.

At this point, Danny Doormat tried to keep the peace: "I think what Mr. Step means…"

We both ignored him and tore back into each other.

NOTE: I think this would be a good time to remind you that all of this wasted time, hostility and drama was for ONE student who I could have easily just allowed the system to push through. Remember kiddies: Caring = more drama. Apathy = under the radar.

After a comment I shan't repeat, (which the counselor tried his best not to hear) step-mom not so subtly implied, that "maybe something else was going on here." **—RACISM**

Finally, she threw a few more verrrry specific accusations at me regarding my classroom behavior which I can only assume (since she never sat in on my class) came from the mouth of her loving son, that paragon of honesty and citizenship (with 30 discipline referrals and multiple epic fails.)

> Slander (n.) *slan*dur*-oral defamation, in which someone tells one or more persons an untruth about another which untruth will harm the reputation of the person defamed. Slander is a civil wrong (tort) and can be the basis for a lawsuit.

Just thought I'd mention that, but I digress…

Since I had made a promise to step-mom (and, more importantly, myself) to do what was best for her kid, I still offered to accept the re-written paper paragraph by paragraph and correct it (like should have been done during the previous WEEK in class,) and reminded her that the grade didn't matter because, as I have repeated several *thousand* times, the school was going to 'round up' her final grade and pass her anyway.

I know, I know, you don't have to say it.

I'm as disgusted as you are that this is what I have sunk to, accepting late work (that will take significant time on *my* part to grade) from a cheater and a liar to placate a narrow-minded pseudo-parent that was now playing tough—"he's going to write TWO paragraphs a night!"—and the infantry of enablers that made this all possible. AND I got the joy of watching self-righteous little Willy sit in class with a big smile on his face like he somehow won the battle to perpetuate his own unique brand of inherited ignorance.

As of the writing of this chapter, he just turned in his first two paragraphs. They were, to put it mildly, in need of work, and the paper was formatted improperly.

Step-mom clearly isn't as "hands on" as promised, huh? She's probably busy not checking her Emails.

As for the "guidance" counselor?

Approached me the next day, told me he wasn't happy with the way the meeting went; I thought he was going to apologize for not intervening more and "having my back" more assertively.

Wrong. He told me:

1. *I* was the reason the meeting went south.
2. *The parent* didn't want to hear about the "50 no matter the effort" policy.
3. *We* have to do what's in the best interest of the kids, and
4. *I* might not like to hear it, but "the parents are in charge."

That, ladies and gentlemen, is **ENABLEMENT.**

I haven't been that angry in quite some time. I contemplated pulling his spine out until I realized I'd probably come up empty. I asked him to leave.

He suggested "we should get together and talk about 'getting on the same page' when I wasn't so upset."

Sorry, Danny but, to quote Brad Pitt's Achilles *"there are no pacts between lions and men."*

1. I should never have been asked to endure that meeting in the *first* place.
2. It's not my job to tell the parents what they "want," it's my job to tell them what they "need." (And since when do you speak for every parent in the world?)
3. I teach my students like I parent my children, and if anyone

thinks that "isn't in the best interest of the student," then you and I are different *species*.

4. Parents are not "in charge" (of me, anyway.) They pay taxes and vote for budgets and sit on school boards, but they are only one voice in the village involved in educating their children.

I could go on and on and on and on, but why?

Let's leave it at this. The "Four Horsemen" exist, and they are spreading like the war and pestilence of their eponymous Biblical forebears. Again, I urge parents, guardians, ANYbody actually, that cares about their kids—

Search your heart. Not your ego, or your anger, your HEART. *Let go of your stereotypes and previous encounters like you expect me to do when I engage your child.* And if, <u>after making an **informed** decision based on **both** sides of the story,</u> you truly think that I am doing my best to teach your child, then "judge not that ye be not judged."

I like that. I should write that down somewhere.*

*Kidding, of course.

Epilogue: White or Wrong.

Shortly after this chapter was "in the can" several students (of, ironically, myriad backgrounds) sent me a video link wherein the Dartmouth-educated, African-American president of the Chicago teachers union made some potentially incendiary (and, by my assessment, unnecessary) comments about how white people were to blame for the failure of schools in her area.

Sad. Especially since the gist of her argument was something I fundamentally agree with; however, crying racism has become the contemporary equivalent of crying "Witch" in Salem, Massachusetts in the late 1600s—and it's every bit as frivolous and irresponsible now as it was then. Calling someone racist has become almost like calling someone a child molester, where the accused is already branded and, if they argue vehemently, look guilty. If they don't argue, they're assumed to be guilty *without remorse*. For this one instance I will forego my promise of zero profanity because there is no other way to respond to this but to say:

Bullllllllllllllllllllllllllllllshit.

The aforementioned union president, Ms. Karen Lewis, is obviously a well-educated woman, and the fact that she felt the need to "play to the house" was particularly disappointing because her main argument was lost in her reach for memorable shock value.

Ms. Lewis continually referred, exclusively, to "black and brown" children when she expressed concern for students that were being adversely affected, asking *"When will there be an honest conversation about the poverty, racism and inequality that hinders the delivery of a quality education product in our school system?"* Lewis also inquired *"When will we address the fact that rich, white people think they know what's in the best interest of children of African Americans and Latinos…?"* She furthermore felt enabled to speak for *the entire white population* of her district saying *"[they] don't want to pay for the education of poor black and brown children."* And that *"we don't want to say that out loud."*

While I was very proud that my former students all saw the hypocrisy and flawed logic in Ms. Lewis' commentary, I felt compelled to comment on this as an addendum to the previous chapter in light of the obvious connection.

I'm going to look past the obvious misinterpretation of what President Lewis actually MEANT (venture capitalists claim to want what's best for black and brown kids...they don't) and focus on what she actually SAYS, which is cause for concern. First of all, Ms. Lewis asks "when are we going to have an honest conversation about... poverty, racism, and inequality..?" Probably as soon as we have an honest conversation that NOT every poor child being affected by this is black or brown. There are, last I checked, plenty of poor white and Asian kids in Chicago (and elsewhere.)

She also says, and I quote: "Rich white people think they know what's in the best interest of children of African American and Latinos..." I'll spare her the grammatical correction and instead ask the obvious question: What would happen if I (a white teacher and author) said, in a public forum, "poor black and Latino kids are falling behind their peers because what I teach them isn't reinforced or valued at home?" We all know the answer to that; therefore, and the fact that Ms. Lewis hasn't been metaphorically drawn and quartered speaks to blatant reverse discrimination, does it not?

Finally, she feels enabled to speak for the entire white population of her district saying "[they] don't want to pay for the education of poor black and brown children." And that "we don't want to say that out loud" prior to portraying herself (an obviously well-educated, affluent African-American woman) as having been able to eavesdrop on "secret white conversations" as proof because "people didn't know exactly who [she] was."

OK...this vitriol has to stop. I have had scathingly raw, honest conversations with my students for 25 years now, and I KNOW what is said, in each community, about the other ones. Some of it is good, some of it is bad. As I echoed earlier, racism and bigotry exist, IN ALL DIRECTIONS, and probably always will, with no group holding exclusive rights to them. Please, let's stop using racism as the go-to trump card for EVERY argument that one doesn't have enough credible sources/valid statistics to win, shall we?

The sad part is, _I agree with the general premise of this woman's argument_—that rich venture investors are making a ton of money pretending to care about what's in the best interest of kids they can't even REMOTELY relate to. (I **wrote** about that **exact** issue in the "Data deity" chapter of THIS BOOK, for God's sake!) But she lost me when she started painting with the broad "black and brown = poor and white = rich" brush. I grew up in Fishtown, Philadelphia and I'd be willing to wager that my upbringing was every bit as "hood" (or more) than Karen Lewis' ever was. That being said, I'm going to refrain from what could have been an epic retaliatory assault on this woman, and instead <u>call on our educational "leaders" to drop the race card and start talking about our kids in the *collective* sense, because THEY are going to run OUR world someday—period.</u> Our children don't do what we say, they do what we do, so it is incumbent on us—to quote Mahatma Gandhi—to "be the change [we] wish to see in the world."

SECTION 2
A Few Treasures From My Own Private Vault.

"Illumination comes so hard, makes me see but leaves its scars
At times I wish that I didn't know, what I know now."

—Rollins Band

Like almost any teacher, I am confronted by a never ending wave of forces designed to make my job singularly difficult. I've already touched briefly on the parent problem, but sometimes the assault comes from high above, sometimes it comes from within the machine, and sometimes it comes from the peers you *thought* you were fighting the tide with together.

Allow me, once again, to elaborate…

Hexpectations

Every person that works at a school *loves* orientation day; teachers love it most of all. Seriously, who *wouldn't* love coming back to school to hear about all of the hard work our (12 month employed) leaders have been doing, and all the groundbreaking programs they've facilitated for us, all designed to really, truly, improve the quality of our children's' education?

HAhAhAHaHaHAhaHAhaHAHahAhaHaHAhAhahaHAhAha HAhaHA.

I imagine, I would *love to believe*, that at one time it was like that. These days, when we are all asked to file into the auditorium/cafeteria/wherever on that first day back, I imagine most teachers feel like saying "why are these people speaking German, and why do those showers look suspicious?"

Our new Superintention, (no, I didn't spell it wrong; *think* about it) whom everyone agreed looked like the yellow M&M from the television advertisements, greeted us with the proclamation that she had two words for us, and one of those words was "high expectations."

…and **one** of those words was <u>high</u> <u>expectations</u>.

It got progressively worse from there.

Thank goodness we, the teachers and administrators didn't have HEXPECTATIONS* because what we got dumped on us *the day before students arrived for the first day of school* almost rendered me speechless with its level of ineptitude.

Almost.

After the usual caffeine and carbohydrate overloading that accompanies our return from Summer "vacation" (also known as working our second or third jobs to supplement our teaching income,) we were ushered into the auditorium for the pre-game, rah-rah, *thisyearisgonnabegreatrightupuntilwescrewyouover* speech. Basically, a bunch of people who were very much aware that teachers and students *were coming back*, in exactly 2 months, were going to demonstrate how inadequately they prepared for that moment during their two months of PAID employment.

Then we broke into groups to find out all the new changes that we were going to be expected to learn, master, and employ starting **tomorrow**, with **your children**.

Teachers of America! Put your hands up if this sounds familiar to you!

Damn. That's a lot of hands. *(P.S. If you actually put your hand up while reading this, you totally rock, and you have made this crappy author very happy.)*

Off to the cafeteria, where we were then alerted to the fact that we had a NEW computer system (our third in four years,) the *teachers* were given 30 minutes, on computers that continually lost their [*kind-of-**important***] internet connections, to learn an ENTIRELY NEW COMPUTER SYSTEM. The computer system that would control grades, discipline referrals, contact with parents, inter-office communications, and so much more.

In 30 minutes,

on computers that kept logging off due to our horrible bandwidth, which we complain about every year.

In fairness, the building administrators had it worse than the teachers—a 2 hour class *on the new computer system*, in one room, WITH NO COMPUTERS.

You simply cannot make this stuff up.

Ok, off to our various departments (in my case the English Department,) which is usually a pretty good time, as we are reunited with our kindred spirits to talk shop about stuff we know, and share ideas about stuff we've discovered over the Summer.

Usually.

Today we were greeted by a—I kid you not—close to 100 pg. bound edition of the new curriculum we were supposed to read, *internalize* and ***begin implementing into our lessons THE NEXT DAY.***

I guess I could go into some more metaphorical comparisons of what this would be like in any other profession (medical, military, accounting, engineering, etc.) and the potentially tragic results, but I'll just take a minute and let that sink in.

The message was becoming clear:

- We KNOW you create, tweak, update and adjust your lessons over the 2+ MONTHS you're away in the summer.
- We KNEW you were coming back **on this date**, but
- We chose to wait **until the day before the students came back** to change your rooms around, introduce you to our new computer system (which is still filled with glitches,) and ask you to learn and implement a massive, impractical, as-yet-untested curriculum OVERNIGHT.

Oh, and by the way, your ability to implement this nonsense will be paramount in our State's new teacher evaluation system! (More on **that** little slice of Hell later.)

...oh yeah, and the materials like pencils, pens, board markers, and some of those books you wanted? We ordered them late so they'll be in around Halloween. Sorry, but we were busy <u>practicing advanced yoga.</u> *

*You're pretty smart, reader, so I think you know what I'm saying...

The *underlying* message was becoming crystal clear.
- We do not care about you.

Of course, this is nothing new. Schools are, with frighteningly increasing regularity, run by people increasingly out of touch with the students *within* them. Like the bumper sticker says: "THOSE THAT CAN, TEACH; THOSE THAT CANNOT PASS LAWS ABOUT TEACHING."

Never was this type of disparity more evident than here, in school, the day before 1,500 + eager (well, most of 'em, anyway) minds returned in the hopes that we had gotten it right while they were away. Ready to learn if we could just show them that we cared enough to break free from the status quo and, instead, used our time to prepare for their return by putting the same time and effort into their returns as we ask them to put into research papers and projects.

But no, they'll come back tomorrow to a screwed up computer system, no materials (unless I run out to Staples and buy my own,) and a teaching staff more confused than the Pope at a Venom concert and under more pressure than Mount Fuji.

But we'll have *high expectations!* (Wait…never mind, they get half credit for doing nothing.) Well, at least we'll teach them *account-ability!* (Wait…never mind, we have about 60 new exceptions built into every nook and cranny of our "discipline" code, *another* little wrinkle presented to us today.) Oh, for Pete's sake…at least we can sit them down and read with them (Wait…never mind, the books you ordered *back in April/May* haven't arrived yet?)

I could go on and on, but why?

Just understand this, and understand it <u>clearly</u>:

There are a whole lot of teachers and educational support staff, at every level, *putting their jobs on the line, trying* to teach your children to the best of their abilities *in spite of* , (and sometimes in direct opposition to,) what sometimes feels like a conspiracy of fools trying to *prevent* them from doing just that.

Epilogue:
What the Hex are you talking about, Step?
A personal note on "Hexpectations"

I'm hoping to start a little secret revolution among the educational community!

- Since high expectations is/are, according to the walking brain dead, *one word* now,
- and since the utter ridiculousness of that gesture mimics the utter ridiculousness associated with those alleged "high expectations,"
- I suggest we use the word HEXPECTATIONS to mock the morons
- who claim to *encourage* them but *understand* true high expectations for students the way the President understands being homeless. *Hexpectations*, people, spread the word.

A [Reading] Deal With the Devil

Whether you know it or not, you all know the basic elements of the archetypical Faust story.

You do, really.

Here, I'll show you. Can you think of any stories where the main character wants something that he/she can't have, so they call on the devil (or someone symbolizing the devil,) make the deal, and they are either damned or saved, depending on how the story ends?

Movies: *The Little Mermaid, The Devil's Advocate, Click, Star Wars III, BeDazzled, etc.*

Comic books: *Ghost Rider, Spawn, Necromancer, etc.*

Books: *Dr. Faustus, Picture of Dorian Gray, The Devil and Tom Walker, etc.*

Yes, everything from *The Devil and Homer Simpson* to *The Devil Went down to Georgia,* from poetry to art, opera to manga, takes us back to that timeless tale of makin' deals with the Lord of the Lies; and you know one thing most of those stories have in common?

A contract.

Be it a handshake or an agreement signed in blood, the accepting of a gift to the passing of a curse, the damned all seal their fate by engaging in some sort of contract that binds them in blood to their Satanic Majesty.

Anyone who has ever attended a mortgage closure or signed a marriage license knows how this feels. (**Thank God my wife never reads my books.)**

But enough about God! We're here to talk about the enemy, the bad guy, the tempter of the weak and destroyer of souls, The Big D...

and his **contract**—guaranteed to sound like a *great idea at the time* but , (sure as the San Jose Sharks will choke in the playoffs,) it will damn you in the end.

At this point I can hear you mumbling to yourself: "Is this chapter even remotely related to education, Step?" Of course it is, I just *taught* you about Faust stories, darn it, so be patient.

Because now I'm going to tell you how to destroy a child's love of reading.

Actually, that's not totally true. I'm going to give you two approaches that were tried with our kids, mine (developed over 24 years of trying to get thousands and thousands of kids, including my own, to read) and the one suggested by what I can only describe as a conglomerate of administrators interested in "making us a reading-centric (whatever *that* is) district." I'm not going to tell you which is which, but I want you to ...

and be honest, now,

tell me which one makes YOU want to read more.

Then I'll tell you how things worked out.

I know, I know, some of you love to read already; some of you— and, to be honest, you're probably the majority—don't read. If you're in the latter group, I'm sorry for whatever forces made you stop liking reading, and I wish I could have been your teacher and fixed that, but I still want your opinion, ok?

OK, let's get ready to rumble.

In one corner, we have the BLUE Rock 'Em Sock 'Em Robot, approach #1—Keep a bunch of books in the classroom for the kids to look at and check out, take the students to the library once in a while for a bigger selection. Let them *see* you reading, *talk* to them about what you're reading. Lend out books, don't care if you get them back, but if you do, *talk* to the kids about what they thought, and tell 'em you can get them more books like the ones they like (and then *do* it.) *Get to know* your kids and bring in books that you think *one particular kid* might like; even if they were hesitant, that kind of individual attention works wonders. Read (really read, don't just skim) anything a student gives you that they think is really profound—you'll learn a lot about the kid and make them feel both empowered and not alone. *Post* what you're reading, *admit* that you neither like nor understand all of the stuff you read. *Share* some of the shorter works, poems, articles, etc. with the class as in-class assignments. **NOTE: It is amazing how kids can read text "above" their "reading levels" if it's stuff related to them or things they're interested in.** Be infectious, love reading unabashedly and they'll be willing to try it, but don't try to promote something you don't really love; they can *smell* insincerity, and that only fuels their disinterest.

And speaking of promoting something you don't really love…

In the other corner, we have the RED Rock 'Em Sock 'Em Robot, approach #2—Mandate that every student gets a copy of this document, and returns it signed (in BLOOD! just kidding…)

JOIN THE WE LOVE READING MOVEMENT!
Love of Reading Student Contract—Secondary.

How many of you saw that word "contract" and went "Uh oh..?" *Nice. That means you're paying attention.*

I can't (and even if I could, I wouldn't) bore you with the entire, exhaustive document, but I can and will tell you that it asks the student, parent, English teacher, and Satan himself (again, kidding, sorry…) to sign a contract agreeing to turn off all distractions (computers, phones, games, TVs, radios, etc.) read for 20 minutes or more a day, think and talk about each book afterwards, and MAINTAIN ACCURATE LOG SHEETS OF EVERYTHING YOU READ: WHERE, WHEN, HOW MUCH, ETC. [which would, according to contract, be collected by, analyzed by, and discussed with, the aforementioned English teacher.]

OK…go back and read 'em again. Let me know which one would

make YOU want to read more and, if you're a parent, which one would you rather your kid be subjected to? Be honest.

If, in your imaginary battle, the Blue Rock 'Em Sock 'Em robot won by knockout, please continue reading, and know that a 25 year English teacher [and father of four readers] supports your decision. If you liked the second approach, I admire your honesty but I must categorically disagree with you.

And I'll tell you why.

When my students came to me, on fire, about the *still-warm-from-the-copier-and-available-in-three-languages-so-as-to-be-politically-correct* reading contracts, I did what good teachers do,

I listened.

That might be nuclear-grade important, so I'll say it again—

I did what good teachers do—

I *listened.*

My kids told me that there was no way they were doing this thing, wondered "who the [heck] designed [it?]" and led the witness by asking "Step, you can't possibly [support] this [ill-advised reading contract!]"

Mini-punctuation lesson! When you use brackets [ ] in a quotation, that means that the speaker didn't actually say *those <u>exact</u> words* but the words used in the brackets are more appropriate to the clarity of the statement.

Like if you asked me in an interview why I changed certain words in the book and I said "I swore to complete *Teaching Sucks But We Love It* with no profanity,"

you could just type:

Step said "[he] swore to complete [it] with no profanity" and you'd be good,

AND you'd understand why I had to change some of my students' comments for publication purposes!

They were, understandably, indignant and offended; after all, *I taught them*, so they're pretty keen at picking up on things that smell like bad voodoo.

Apparently, many of my brothas and sistas teaching at _____High School were doing the same voodoo I do, too (that is, teaching *real, **life-long*** reading skills) because if you drew a pie chart of how many of our kids liked this LOVE of READING MOVEMENT, the "we love it" slice would look like a splinter getting devoured by an obese Pac Man.

Apparently, the idea of having to stop in the middle of reading something interesting and record the experience (and the pages) in detail didn't sit well with our teenage literati.

One student, Odin bless him, exclaimed that *"nobody would ever want to drive if they had to stop at the [expletive] DMV every time they wanted to get behind the wheel!"*

…and people think teenagers are stupid.

Once I was done listening to their fire and brimstone rants, I asked them how many of them would read more if we "did the contract thing?"

ZERO (out of 112)

"Okaaaay…well, how many of you would want to read *less* if we did [it]?"

67 (out of 112) …and bonus points for YOU if you caught the proper use of brackets!

I was desperately trying to find *something* of value in this Satanic document (because I already knew damn well I wasn't going to do it) so that when I was called up on charges of insubordination I could say I tried my best to find a shred of evidence that it was a good idea. Two strikes, final pitch:

"OK, now—and be honest—how many of you will cheat or lie when you tell me how much you read in your reading logs?"

"You mean like with the Summer Reading, when we all waited to the last day of the Summer and just wrote in a bunch of fake times and pages? Like that?"

SteeeeeeeeeeeeRIKE three.

Listen, folks, when every single kid tells me that they wouldn't read more if we were to do something, and over HALF of them say they would read *less*, then I ain't doing it. Thank goodness my students were against it like eggs are against sledgehammers (and for roughly the same reason) because I knew in the very depths of my soul that this was wrong.

Now, that may sound a bit hyperbolic coming from me but you have to understand that reading is one of my great passions, and I consider it my **mission** to repair the damage our educational system has done to our kids in making them hate reading; and, if I do say so myself, I'm pretty damn good at it. That having been said, I will adopt *any* strategy that I think might get kids to read, and I have tried some things in my lifetime about which I thought "THIS will be a colossal waste of time" only to be pleasantly surprised when they worked for one or two kids.

Because one or two kids are important enough to try something.

When kids can read, they feel empowered, and when they learn to read beyond basic comprehension, when they learn to see themselves and their world in the literature, and begin to see how all stories are related, well,

I have seen that look; the look when one of my students starts to "get it," and THAT, ladies and gentlemen, is what keeps me doing what I do.

And if somebody could show me a way that would work with every student?

Why, I might just sign a contract…

Faustian foolishness aside, take some advice from your ol' Uncle Step: be wary of any *strategy du jour* or newfangled approaches to reading suddenly (and miraculously) "discovered" *because-somebody-read-something-written-by-someone-probably-designed-to-put-money-in someone-else's pocket.* YOU know your kids, your students, your fledgling readers better than anyone, so if you are faced with an approach that doesn't resonate with you, be cautious. As always, the tried and true methods work the best—if you love it, they will grow to love it, too.

Kids learned to read, and love reading, LONG before any of these BS methodologies and paradigms was inflicted upon us, and all it took was a person that loved reading spending some literary time with a kid.

That method still works, and you can quote me on that. Maybe if we allowed for a little more of that in the classroom instead of all the teaching-toward-testing we are asked/forced to do… But YOU don't have those limitations upon you! **So sit with a kid, *your* kid, or maybe a niece or nephew? Brother or sister? It doesn't matter—just read, and keep reading.**

You'll thank me someday.

But you don't have to.

I could go on and on, but I have an appointment at the Crossroads, at midnight, with a rather sinister-looking gentleman that says he has a way for me, forever, to keep students from confusing *there*, *their*, and *they're*.

I figure it's worth a shot.

"I'll Push In Yours If You Push In Mine."

Sometimes, the reality of the teaching profession is so much stranger than fiction that one can only look upon it and laugh, because if you didn't (as the saying goes) you would cry; sometimes from heartbreak, sometimes from frustration, and sometimes just because the things that are done to us are so profound in their ridiculousness that all you can do *is* laugh.

It's late November, and a pretty sizeable portion of the English teachers have been summoned to a double-secret probation meeting afterschool. Things being what they are, exactly NONE of those people think this is going to be about a Thanksgiving bonus; *ou contraire mon ami*, they're preparing themselves to be stuffed like the turkeys we're treated like. And yet, even their pre-violation preparation could not have prepared them for the classroom cluster bomb that awaited them.

NOTE: Thank Zeus, I was not present at this meeting (which sounded an awful lot like the "hey, guys, we made a teensy weensy error" meeting the workers at Chernobyl attended) but my dark apprentice, Darth Trocious, was there and, as we Sith have a symbiotic relationship, I shall relate the *are-you-kidding-comrade?* details using a combination of his viscous verbiage and my own pedestrian prose:

Translation: *The stuff in italics is him talking,* **the stuff in bold is me filling in the blanks**, because I am **bold**, and he is...*thin, and kind of slanty*, if you must know.

"After some initial pleasantries and apologies (read: lubing and awkward pillow talk) we learned, right off the bat, that we were being shuffled, in LATE NOVEMBER, like a hot deck at the Bellagio. Funds had been used improperly and, because of that, teachers that [had]spent <u>*the last 4 months*</u> *teaching, learning, and developing relationships*

with their students, [were] going to be uprooted IMMEDIATELY and [tossed around] to different classrooms. Some of the teachers won't even be 'teachers' for the rest of the year, they will be assistants to other English teachers who, themselves, will now be saddled with new classrooms filled with kids they don't know at all."

I can hear you from here going "Wait…what??"

Allow me to explain, in as simple terms as a screw-up of this magnitude will allow, how this classroom carnage (and the damage it did to so many students' educations) was created.

1. Title 1 funds are allocated to districts with a highly impoverished population, like ours.
2. Those funds are supposed to be used to assist the "at-risk" students in some way, usually in the form of a class geared towards basic skills and improvement thereof.
3. The school got these funds and used them to assist in paying salaries of teachers who, at the time of their hiring, were asked to teach the "low level (or whatever YOU want to call 'em) students."

THE PROBLEM: "Outreach" (our school's euphemism for lower level) classes are (according to the suits) just *versions* of a normal class: required English. *That is NOT how Title 1 funds are meant to be used*; they are expected to create non-required SUPPLEMENTAL courses or programs for the "at-risk" students.

THE PLOT THICKENS: The aforementioned teachers (who are told NOTHING about financial allocations and such nonsense) are being paid (by nimrods who are SUPPOSED to know about financial allocations and such nonsense) from funds that require that they teach something *totally* different.

…AND THICKENS SOME MORE: We got audited, which is to say the morons that didn't know how to spend Title 1 money got audited. According to the ~~stormtroopers~~ auditors, "Outreach" classes are not "supplemental assistance" to "at-risk" kids; thus, the teachers whose paychecks are being signed by Title 1 must, in fact, be placed into actual supplemental assistance.

BUT... **STAY WITH ME NOW, BECAUSE THERE IS MATH INVOLVED HERE:** *this Title 1 money only makes up a percentage of our pay, and that percentage is commensurate to the percentage of classes we teach that meet Title 1 (or supposed to be Title 1) classes.*

Whhhhaaaaaat?????

For example, I myself had (Key word: HAD) two "Outreach" classes out of five classes total. So 40% of my check comes from Title 1. Therefore, 40% of my class assignment has to become "supplemental assistance."

I'll say this BOLDLY, as it might be important in the context of how utterly ridiculous this is:

...so the school has to *invent* Title 1 appropriate courses for us to teach; in late NOVEMBER.

THAT means that the "at risk" students we're currently teaching must be pushed onto someone ELSE so that we can teach this SUPPLEMENT!

My two "low level" classes are mine no more. One will be dissolved into other classes, and the students therein shoveled around and mixed into all new schedules and classes. The other will be taken over by Ms. Stronzate, who is losing a 90 minute block class of her own, taking my 1 class, and taking on two supplement courses, which the administration has chosen to call...

<u>wait</u> for it...

"push-in" classes.

Staggeringly appropriate, given the prison rape *je ne ses quoi* of the events.

But back to the fallout for my young apprentice...

So I teach two "Push-In" classes of "at risk" kids, and then Ms. Cucumber teaches two "Push-Ins", which means Mr. Granary has to take her two senior classes, and he ALSO teaches a "Push-In", which means he loses his two sophomore classes, which means those kids are dissolved into other classes belonging to Ms. Kobra, Ms. Habenero, and Mr. Gumballs.

Got all that?

Probably not, so I again turn to Darth Trocious, who will summarize this whole" push-in enigma" for y'all. Take it away, Trocious:

*Simply put, in English classes alone, **four teachers** were moved to this mystical "push in teaching assignment," more than **ten teachers** had multiple classes drastically altered to accommodate all the moving around, and that directly led to disruption, confusion, and discomfort for literally **HUNDREDS of students,** ALL of whom would be expected to perform at a high level on myriad tests that (apparently) couldn't make the process any easier by ascertaining which of them needs HELP!"*

Ready for the best part? The administration that called this meeting had NO CLUE what a "push-In" class is, and, to add insult to injury…
waaaaaiiiit **for it…**

THEY DON'T KNOW WHO THE "AT-RISK" KIDS ARE!!!!

They even suggested, (with that same look the Chernobyl directors gave their soon-to-be-two-headed employees) that maybe teachers could double secret E-mail them with *suggestions* of what kids may be "At-risk!"

HAHahAhaHahAHAhaHAhaaHahAHAha…sniff, ha.

Sooooooo, let me get this straight: <u>DUE TO YOUR OWN ERROR</u> (or misappropriation of funding), <u>you are moving your teachers around like pawns on a Chessboard,</u> <u>blowing up classes,</u> <u>pairing people up that may or may not be compatible,</u> <u>and doing this all for kids you can't identify?</u>

*And you're doing this all **immediately**, in **LATE NOVEMBER?***

Yeah, that'll work.

Clearly in the best interest of the kids, too.

In the meantime, let's see:

- You have inundated these kids with a never-ending battery of BS testing (that we, the teachers, of course, have to give them.)
- We, the teachers, have had to compile and calculate all that data (effectively, doing YOUR JOB **FOR** YOU,) and yet
- You can't figure out which kids are "at risk?"

I have a question.

It's a small one.

WHAT THE (string of expletives) **ARE YOU** (more expletives) **MORONS DOING WITH ALL OF THE** (even more expletives, sorry, I'm really angry **) DATA YOU DEMAND FROM THESE POOR KIDS???**

I don't know why I'm shocked. The people we pay to do nothing BUT manage the money can't figure out how to properly appropriate the funding we receive, so why should the people we pay to analyze data know what the hell *they're* doing? But these are the tools in charge, folks.

Can you imagine if this kind of thinking extended beyond the school? It would be like putting the same bankers that ran the country into apocalyptic debt in charge of the money for the "recovery."

Thank God we're not that stupid...

All we're doing is ruining the education of a bunch of kids, and making a few good teachers want to quit the profession.

Something is getting "pushed-In," that's for damn sure.

Of course, ***their*** lack of preparation constitutes ***our*** emergency, so Operation Divide and Conquer happens *in two days*, or three, maybe after we get back from Thanksgiving break.

Who knows.

Not them; and it hurts me, for real, to know that this is "business as usual" in school districts across the country. But, of course, the uninformed public will go on blaming teachers for not being able to properly educate their kids, never knowing that we're having something else entirely "pushed in" while we're trying to do just that.

Sometimes you just have to laugh.

"I Don't O.W.E You Nothing."

One of the coolest things about having two books [about teaching] published is the support, advice, and cool information I get from teachers nationwide.

One of the saddest things about it is the stories I get from those same people about how, when they attempt to elevate the profession and those around them, they are stabbed in the back and left hanging in the breeze by their jealous, petty, and far too complacent peers.

Yeah, I know a little about that, but I never thought about including it in this book until a "colleague" of mine grabbed me in the hall last week and told me *"[she] heard great things about [my second] book."*

"Thanks a lot, that's very cool. Thank you" was my standard reply.

"Do you think I could read it?"

"Um…I know they have a couple copies in the school library, but they're usually out. I'm getting a few in next week; do you want me to let you know when…"

She cut me off—*"What is this, some kind of sales pitch?"*

"Excuse me?" I countered, having been surprisingly cut off in mid answer.

"You want me to buy a copy of your book, is that it?"

"If you'd like to, that would be great. I can get it for you cheaper than online, and I'll even sign it for you, and…"

"Oh," (sarcastically) *how **nice** of you."*

"…of course," I finished, through gritted teeth, "as I said, there are copies in the libr—"

"I don't need your book, and I don't owe you nothing. I was doing you a favor by—"

My turn to interrupt: "By doing what? Asking for a free copy of a book that strangers, friends, peers, students, and FAMILY MEMBERS paid for? I appreciate the nice words about the book, but nobody ever said you were obligated to—"

"I don't owe you nothing!" she repeated.

Deep breath, exhale,) "No, you don't owe me ANYthing, except the last two minutes of my life back, because I just wasted them talking to you and your obvious {censored} issues. I am profoundly stupider and sadder for having spent time with you, but that's ok, because you've given me some material for the *next* book you won't read."

Damn, I thought, I'm trying to tell the stories, let the world know what we're going through, promote the positive aspects of our profession, AND put myself in the crosshairs doing it. But you don't want to help, contribute, or promote my books?

I would love to tell you I let that conversation pass like gas into the ether of my mind, but I didn't. I remained angry and confused at the perception that anyone owed me anything for simply telling other people about our common frustrations/adventures. The more I thought about that word—owe—it became an obvious acronym in my mind. OWE…own worst enemy. Sometimes, as teachers, we are just that.

Listen folks, I love when people ask me "how is the new book coming?" And I certainly don't mind when people offer suggestions about what should go *into* the books, even if these "ghost writers" are basically encouraging me to put *my* ass on the line to tell the world our [collective] story. I don't even mind when people take credit for things that show up in the books, and I've heard some interesting claims from my alleged "co-writers" (usually people that were nowhere to be found when the work was being done or the heat was coming down.)

That having been said, I **do** mind when, after all the questioning, probing and suggesting, someone off handedly tells me "oh I didn't read your book; I don't read books."

Really? Thanks for the support.

If one of my co-workers started an organic wheat grass restaurant, I'd find a way to support it, because they're my **colleagues.**

Not to beat a dead horse, but in the last 3 years I have published two books, (one of which has topped the Amazon list under "teachers" for almost three years,) been featured in newspapers, magazines, etc. You'd think "English teacher, *wrote a few books*, got some local and national attention, might be something we should promote as a school, right?"

Wrong.

I can understand that to a degree; after all, the material in those books might make some of the people in question uncomfortable.

Good. It was supposed to.

However, I *couldn't get 25% of* **the ENGLISH Department in my own school** *to read the books or write online reviews.* Sometimes, it gets a little frustrating trying to speak up for a group of people that won't even support one of their own, particularly when I have to listen to the incessant drone of *"[the public] doesn't understand what we go through"* and *"someone should say something"* from the same people.

I could give you, literally, a hundred stories from teachers across this great land of ours that illustrate how we, as teachers, sometimes throw each other under the school bus. Instead, I'm going to risk flattening the soapbox by getting my big ass right up on it for a moment. This goes out to all my brothers and sisters out there—teachers, subs, administrators, food services, counselors, assistant staff, EVERYbody whose job it is to educate and accommodate our young people:

STOP

FIGHTING

EACH OTHER.

We already have an ever-increasing wave of people downgrading, disrespecting and destroying our profession (most of which don't know a damn thing about us) without us tearing each other apart from within. Don't be our **own worst Enemy.**

Some hindsight from your author dude

As I went through the proofreading process, re-reading this chapter [months after writing it,] I'm not ashamed to admit that I was embarrassed. Sounded a bit like a petulant child.

In need of a good smack, I was.

But I kept it, as is, (or was?) because the venom was authentic when I spat it, and because I still feel like that from time to time.

I suspect that most teachers feel that way when their 'comrades' (you know the ones) laughingly profess "Oh, I *never* take work *home*"

and then ask

"can I 'borrow' that 4 week unit and all the materials that you created from scratch so I can coast like a brainless jellyfish for the next month? Oh, and do you have the handouts that go with it, or do I have to get someone to photocopy those *myself?*"

If you're a decent teacher (or a decent worker in just about any profession,) SOMEbody's name is in your head right now.

If you can't think of anyone—***you're*** probably the person in need of repair, so (God forbid) take work *home*, do your *own* legwork, and try to *care* about your job once in a while.

…oh, and buy a freakin' book, will ya? The money goes to charity and you should probably read more anyway.

Lesson Plans—The Good, The Bad, and The Uggly

Yet another joy of being a teacher in this day and age are the never-ending ways that the brainless invertebrates in the big offices (you know, those ones FAR, far away from the actual classrooms) "improve" the way we teachers do our jobs. Kind of like the way politicians and high ranking military officers, from the comfort of air-conditioned offices, "improve" the way soldiers getting shot at do theirs. One of the many ways these clueless jellyfish help us is by changing the format and requirements of the lesson plans oh...I don't know...THREE TIMES in THREE MONTHS.

I'm not going to assume that you know the normal mind-numbing minutiae that goes into writing standard lesson plans (and thereby know why this is so infuriatingly wasteful,) so allow me to elaborate with an oh so subtle simile:

Lesson plans are like blueprints for a construction team (if you had to list exactly what you would be demolishing, framing, build-ing, installing, etc. **every minute, on the minute**, whilst also listing who you would speak to, work with, high-five and drink coffee with during your non-constructional time. We'll also need to know where your building techniques come from and what angles you'll be cut-ting on today and what brand of reciprocating saw you'll be using to make those cuts and...

OK, that wasn't so subtle, but it was accurate. Let me give you the fast and furious overview of these plans and their intended purpose: All teachers are responsible for submitting lesson plans to our admin-istrators, who then pretend to look at them.

Just kidding (not really,) but more on that later.

Anyway, our lesson plans are *supposed* to lay out what we will do every day with our students, much the same way doctors con-struct a plan of care or how construction foremen submit building plans, etc.; therefore, **constantly changing the format** *of our lesson* plans, **making them ever more extensive and micromanaged**, *does nothing but promote confusion and take away from actual time spent preparing interesting, quality lessons*. Because of this, many teachers "cut and paste" lessons, or borrow other teachers', or simply enter plans that have no bearing on what they're actually doing in class and then hope they don't get observed that week. Say it with me, folks: Colossal waste of time and energy.

I have done all of the aforementioned things and more. In fact, when one administrator (let's call him Agent Smith) facilitated *our third change in lesson plan format* **in three months**, I took an unapologetic shot at his credibility as an "educational leader" when I submitted a recipe for gluten-free muffins in the middle of one of my weekly lesson plans. In return, I received an online confirmation from him that "lessons [were] reviewed and approved."

Apparently, Agent Smith DIDN'T know the muffin plan, the muffin plan, the muffin plan. He didn't know the muffin plan that lived on smart aleck lane. Not surprisingly, "Smith" is no longer involved in that particular facet of our educational paradigm, but if he ever gets to read this book: **You know who you are, you're a tool, and I hope everyone sings "the muffin man" song to you everywhere you go.**
Love and kisses, MISter Anderson.

My editor tells me I'm getting too venomous (and thus jeopardizing my mass-market appeal) so here's a funny, but 100% true, story about how our current lesson plan format falls flat in the face of what I will gently refer to as "teaching reality."

I was teaching a class on the novel *1984* and one of our former administrators (funny how these people are all "no longer with us" isn't it?) came in to formally observe my class. During the lesson, the discussion in class became very intense and ALL of the students were 100% into it (rare) so when they asked me a very direct question about why I taught this book every year, they were stone silent for about 10 minutes (VERY rare) while I spoke my heart to them. I told them how my job, as I saw it, was to teach them to THINK, to QUESTION, and to make them *WANT* AN EDUCATION

- *not* because their parents wanted them to go to college,
- *not* to make me look good (and some administrator happy) by passing some arbitrary test, and
- certainly *not* because someone somewhere said that's what they were **supposed** to do.

I wanted them to educate themselves because they should feel good about themselves, and since they were going to be the people running the world that MY children would inherit, I wanted them to feel competent and self-assured; furthermore, there were an awful lot of people HEAVILY invested in keeping them stupid so, at the very least, I wanted them to get smart enough to **scare the living daylights out of those people**.

I'm not sure exactly how it all came out but that was the gist of it, and I'm not ashamed to say that I had real tears welling up by the time I was done, because I MEANT it, and I was *feeling* it, so I went for it. When I was done, there were about 10 seconds of silence and then— and I swear this on the heads of my children—I received an *ovation* from 22 students that lasted into the bell ringing and several kids made it a point to thank me, passionately, for "keeping it real" and "not being like every other teacher" and "for looking out for [them.]"

That remains one of the most gratifying moments of my entire teaching career.

I was told that my lesson wasn't effective because [it] deviated from the lesson plan to an extreme degree and provided no "closure" or "independent practice."

I have no further comment about that.

Trust me when I tell you this happens often. If you must know, on the day of the "gluten-free muffin plans," I took one of my periods with my 11th grade College prep class and spoke with the students about the presidential debate the night before. The students were filled with meaningful questions that involved their world *beyond the classroom*, and we had a great, spirited discussion that left everyone more informed about partisan politics and more tolerant of one another. Great lesson; unfortunately, that doesn't fit into (insert snobby voice) *properly constructed CP 11 English lesson plans.*

Would you like to see what *does* fit into proper lesson plans? Would you like to see what I had to submit FOR EACH DAY, EACH CLASS, EACH PERIOD? Your wish is my command. Here is a **one day** lesson plan for **one freshmen class** that was studying George Orwell's *Animal Farm:* (<u>do not, under any circumstances, feel compelled to read the whole thing</u>; just get a taste, because even a taste of bull crap is enough for you to get the flavor.) When you're done, I think you'll agree with the teachers of America when we tell you that this is an almost criminal waste of time that could spent doing…well, ANYthing…more productive in the preparation of interesting lessons for your children.

DATE: *December 19th, *****

TOPIC: What "constitutes a reign of terror?"

KEY QUESTION: *WHAT methods of terrorism and propaganda does Napoleon employ to extend his reign of terror on Animal Farm?*

MATERIALS: *Print campaign ads/ YOUtube videos of other campaign ads,* **Animal Farm** *novels, packets that I have generated related to the text and its themes/motifs, 'Deeper Reading' question [based on the Kelly Gallagher model] packets I have created and distributed, SMARTboard notes, various visual aids*

THE HOOK: *You DO understand that everything we're reading can be applied RIGHT NOW, right?*

METHOD: *Focus Lesson (Oral/ Written response to Key Question:) — The students will engage in a PRE-KNOWLEDGE exercise by answering several questions designed to draw text-to-life comparisons to Napoleon's reign. The students will then READ chapter 7 INDEPENDENTLY.*

MODELING: *As per usual, I will MODEL the type of written response I expect (with particular emphasis on proper citation) by answering one of the questions NOT given to the class.*

INDEPENDENT PRACTICE: *The students will then respond to higher order thinking questions related to the aforementioned chapter; as found in pg. 35 of their Animal Farm packet.*

DISCUSSION : *will be animated, dynamic, and [hopefully] passionate and controversial—that might lead to an official debate or two—and will ALWAYS facilitate text-to-text and text-to-life connections designed to hammer home both LOVE OF READING and the awareness that, ultimately, there is only one story.*

CLOSURE: *A short WHAT DID YOU TAKE AWAY FROM THIS CHAPTER response.*

ASSESSMENT and FOLLOW UP: As is often the case, when I return the graded response(s,) I will use student examples as models of excellence, emphasizing what is good about them; thereby providing both positive reinforcement to the students that worked hard and pertinent, student-centered models for those who are struggling.

TECHNOLOGY: *SMARTboard technology, laptop carts, and (w/ teacher permission as applicable to the lesson at hand) the use of smartphone applications, and audio equipment.*

DIFFERENTIATED INSTRUCTION: *I will allow "overtime" for every test/quiz if you need more than the prescribed time. Any student that does NOT take the extra time will earn 2 bonus points on that particular quiz/ test. The first student done with an 80% or better grade will receive 5 bonus points on that particular quiz/test. You will have the opportunity to re-take any quiz/test on the Wednesday immediately following that assignment. You will earn the average score of the two assignments, (Ex: You get a 60 on a quiz, re-take it and earn a 90, you receive a 75 as your final score.) If you are absent or in ISS that day you MUST make it up by the end of that week, probably Friday after school. Any student that does NOT need to re-take an assignment will have time to work on homework/SSR/classwork during the make-up time. ALL material on quizzes/test will be reviewed in class, and most will be reviewed, WORD-FOR-WORD, the day before they are administered; furthermore, study groups will be encouraged and given time to review prior to the quizzes/test ALL homework answers/essays/oral responses will be modeled [by me] MULTIPLE times before you are expected to do them on your own. You are always allowed to move your seat to: get a better view of the notes, hear the instructor better, move away from distraction, etc. There will almost always be "bonus" questions on quizzes/tests/ homework assignments/etc.: students that require "reduced assignments" will not be required to answer them; however, all students will have the opportunity to do so for extra credit. Please note that these are just accommodations for those of you that need a little extra help sometimes. We'll do a lot more stuff (like individual meetings with students that need help and keeping your parents aware of the material via Email, etc.) but THE RESPONSIBILITY IS YOURS*

TO BE THE BEST STUDENT YOU CAN BE; there are still deadlines and rules that must be followed to ensure that you evolve into the kind of students that will excel once you have left this class. We will always meet you half way, but that means you have to meet us half way as well! Fairness does not mean equal, fairness means that everyone gets what he or she needs."

GROUPINGS: *Usually, I will allow the groupings to occur organically so the students can bounce what they've absorbed off of one another—despite [what I think is hypocrisy] our in-service input that "certain groups" need to work in small groups more often—I hope to accomplish several things by this: One, I will sense where the cliques within the group dynamic lay. Two, I will see who the leaders, facilitators, and slackers are within the group. Three, it will afford me the time to actively circulate among the groups or meet with individual students that need my help.*

RUBRIC: (Here I had to attach a document showing the rubric I used for this particular assignment.) *Also, please feel free to stop by my class for an oversight of the rubrics I use (many of which are in constant flux as I allow student input to enhance their pertinence,)*

STANDARDS* and HOMEWORK: Here is where we have to attach state standards. I'll give you a quick example:

3.5.12 A—Building upon knowledge and skills gained in preceding grades, by the end of Grade 12, students will: 1.Understand that messages are representations of social reality and vary by historic time periods and parts of the world...

That's ONE standard, from a list that looks like War and Peace.*
   *Believe me; you <u>don't</u> want to hear about <u>how we have to list ALL the</u>

state standards we are covering with EACH lesson; if you thought THIS was boring and a waste of time...

Sorry about that, but I needed you to feel just a bit of my pain before I continued;
meanwhile, back in the actual classroom, where actual learning might take place:

You know what they say about good intentions...

Here's how the ACTUAL "Animal Farm" lesson went:

I spent the first 10 minutes of class explaining why the world was NOT going to end on Dec. 21st (as per the "Mayan calendar scare" of 2012.) I quite literally had to explain to one girl about Leap years not having been factored in and explain the math because she was—*VERY legitimately*—preparing to "do it all" during her "last few days on Erf (her pronunciation.)

I figured it was worth a few minutes of class time to set her straight before she YOLOed her way right into an unwanted pregnancy or a bout of alcohol poisoning for Christmas.

Such are the joys of teaching freshmen.

After the Mayan mathematics lesson, we actually started back into our analysis of *Animal Farm*, comparing the propaganda of the pigs to the political ads the students had brought in to...

Oh, hang on a second, a girl and a boy are fist fighting across the hall and the substitute is calling for help, be right back...

Well THAT took about 15 minutes to get settled, get everyone back [somewhat] on task, call the police, and address the elephant in the room with MY students so they didn't spend the next 45 minutes talking about the fight while I was trying to teach... Ok NOW we can resume, again, our in-depth discussion of *Animal Farm*, with emphasis on how the sheep symbolize the unthinking, obedient hordes of people who blindly obey everything they're told. Serendipitously, in the midst of our discussion, a girl blurts out that she heard from her auntie that "it was so warm out in November 'cause the world was gonna end in a monf."

ALL of the other students inquired, politely, where the [expletive] she was during the first 10 minutes of class, when we covered the non-apocalypse? She laughed and said "I wasn't paying attention," whereupon I replied: "that's too baaaaaaad."

Everyone laughed except her; she didn't get it.

So, back to the *meticulously planned* lesson: after some reading together, identifying some literary techniques (foreshadowing, metaphor) and some actual *thinking* and *stimulating discussion* about the lessons we can learn from Orwell's vision of 'leadership' gone wrong, I had the students do some word association with the characters. This usually generates some interesting action and dialogue. Some of the words we had on the board included LIBERAL, CONSERVATIVE, TYRANT, MANIPULATOR, SPIN DOCTOR, COMPLIANT, and UNEDUCATED. One young lady—when asked to give one word to describe one of the pigs, wrote UGGLY. I politely corrected her that ugly is, in fact, spelled with only one "g."

What followed was a near minute long tirade, a **loud** one, on her part as she told me how *I* was wrong and *"it says right here* [points to the logo on her Ugg boots] *that it be spelled Ugg so UggLY just be that with a 'lee' on the end, and how am I gonna 'come at her neck' like that, etc. etc."*

This is every day, folks. This kind of stuff happens
EVERY
FREAKIN'
DAY in classrooms across this great land of ours.

Normally, I'd squash her and her ignorant posturing faster than a well-informed rhinoceros stepping on a depressingly dumb dandelion, but I was thoroughly enjoying the reactions of her classmates, who were thrilled that someone was—very publicly—announcing to the world that she was…ahem, "less informed"… than they were, at least today. Needless to say, I was verklempt (Yiddish word, look it up) that I was now waaaaaay behind in my *meticulously planned* lesson.

I guess I'll just have to go back, like the people "in charge" (who care so deeply about the quality of our children's education) want me to do and rewrite my lesson plans for the rest of the week to take into account what I didn't touch on today.

Yeah, and if you believe that, I've got some swampland in Uggzebekistan you might be interested in…

SECTION 3
Anti-Teacher America

"Welcome my son, welcome to the machine.
Where have you been? It's alright we know where you've been,
You've been in the pipeline filling in time..."
— *Pink Floyd*

In my early days in the "education business" I told anyone that would listen that the system itself was fundamentally flawed. I have since changed my way of thinking. I am beginning to believe, more and more (and with a stunning amount of textual support) that the educational system in this country is performing *exactly* the way many people want it to perform—very, very badly.

Data has become an entity of worship, and teachers have become scapegoats for an angry, narcissistic generation of kids who—rightfully so—question an outdated system of education that doesn't prepare them for the world that we will soon expect them to inherit. Meanwhile, a small group of people are making a great deal of money investing heavily in the perpetual adolescence of our children, which is facilitated by the incessant testing of our students, the impertinent information we feed to them, and the increasingly anti-teacher sentiment in America. Sadly, very few see the circle designed to chase, and bite, its own tail.

From the front lines, I have witnessed the blatantly devitalizing changes in our contracts, the in-house machinations designed to prevent us from doing our jobs properly, potentially ending in "bad evaluations" for being unable to do what we were *prevented* from doing.

All in all, I grow tired of uninformed citizenry, enabling parents, self-preservation obsessed administrators, and hypocritical politicians citing *teachers* as the primary reason our educational system is failing.

This is roughly the same logic as blaming the tires for the crash of a car that was constructed shoddily, many, many years ago, and chronically "tinkered with" to make it cheaper while compromising safety and efficiency.

Well *this* wheel is getting squeaky, and the noise I make sounds a lot like this:

The **system** sucks.

Please allow me, for a third and final time, to elaborate…

The Data Deity and Its Apathetic Angels

"If something cannot be done to check, or at least modify, our monstrous worship of facts, Art will become sterile, and Beauty will pass away from the land."

—Oscar Wilde

Hey, folks—before we begin this chapter, let me be up front with you the way I am with my students prior to starting a difficult lesson. This particular chapter was, by far, the toughest one to write (my editor is nodding somewhere over whiskey and thorazine.)

HOWEVER, like my difficult classroom lessons, *the really good stuff* lurks within if you stick with me and work though the tough parts. I know this could be considered author suicide telling you that the next 15-20 pages might be rough going, but if you <u>really want to know</u> the issue that teachers nationwide point to as the main "weapon of mass instruction" responsible for destroying education [and our kids] today, then read on, my friend. A very wise man once said that intelligent people make easy things difficult, and wise people make complicated things simple; I will do my best to be the latter.

Ready? Then here we go—

You know why I love little kids? Aside from their obvious tug-at-the-heartstrings cuteness and unconditional love and all that, the thing I find most enchanting about the little ones is that they do not give toss about hurting anyone's feelings in the pursuit of knowledge.

Why is the sun hot? Ok, but why can we feel it from that far away? Ok, but why doesn't it just burn up if it's that hot? Yeah, but why…

This conversation will, if allowed to run its course, inevitably end in the words so many adults are afraid to utter—**I don't know.**

<u>There is absolutely nothing wrong with not knowing.</u>

Confessing to a kid that you need to do some research, in fact, *admitting that, and then involving them in the search for the legitimate answer,* can provide lessons that will stick with a child for life, including:

- The fact that you are not (gasp!) omnipotent, and
- that *admitting* to that is perfectly acceptable; moreover,
- asking questions is, in fact, the single greatest way to educate oneself, but
- once the question is asked, one must be discerning when determining what informational source to use, and whether all of the information contained therein is quantifiable. (This *used* to be known as "don't believe everything you read.")

Now, you must understand, <u>to truly educate someone, you have to get to know them </u>first, <u>find out what they really know and don't know</u>, <u>what they *want* to know</u>, and <u>how hard they will *work* to learn it</u>. <u>You also have to know their background, and what issues </u>(there will be many, and they will be varied) <u>may stand between getting what you *teach* to be something they *understand*</u>. Then <u>you have to work, HARD, to overcome those issues, </u>and <u>prepare for any new ones that may arise throughout the teaching process,</u> **and THAT is why I refer to modern teaching, with no irony whatsoever, as PARENTING WITH A PAYCHECK.**

And that type of education, my friends, takes a LOT of work; it also presumes that you <u>care about the person</u> you're trying to educate.

And that is ***precisely*** why many people support standardized testing and the ever-increasing worship of "educational data"—because they DO NOT want to do that work, and they DO NOT care about students as people. To them, our children are simply test scores and demographics to be monitored, recorded and, if need be, manipulated for their own $elfi$h reaon.

I started seriously writing this book on December 15th, 2012. Four months into the process, a tidal wave of stories broke about cheating scandals related to standardized tests.

In Atlanta, Georgia, Trenton, New Jersey, and Washington, D.C., reports were surfacing that people up and down the food chain, from teachers to principals to chancellors were (allegedly, of course) supervising, or *directly participating in*, the changing of answers, manipulating of data, and other such chicanery, all in the interest of improving test scores for their districts.

I had a few options of how to respond to this:

1. I could vilify the people involved, but there was no need; the national media seemed way ahead of me on that one.
2. I could allow myself to become embittered, knowing that if these people had gotten *caught*, then there were, based on the iceberg principle, many, MANY more people 'under' them engaging in the same type of activity.
3. I could become jaded and simply laugh at the utter ridiculousness of it all, complaining to whomever would listen and posting mad rants on social media like zillions of others.
4. Or I could, and ultimately would, embrace my inner child and ask "**Why?**"

As usual, someone smarter than I am said it more succinctly then I ever could, so I defer to American astrophysicist and science communicator Neil deGrasse Tyson, who observed that *"when students cheat on exams it's because our school system values grades more than students value learning."*

He's 100% correct about THAT, and thanks to nice *sounding* programs like *No Child Left-Behind* and *Race to the Top* we now have people doing whatever it takes to make it look like test scores are going up lest they *lose their jobs* and *have their schools taken over* by the same government that passed those bills.

I'll make it simple for you, folks; those nice *sounding* programs are written by insidious political vipers who DO NOT want to get to know your kids (*especially* those of you in those high risk "urban areas")so they base ALL progress on nice, safe test scores that they can collect from a distance and judge homogeneously from the safety of [their] neighborhoods where schools *don't* need metal detectors but *must* have the latest laptops for every kid.

Oh, and by the way, those same people *don't want* all of the schools to succeed; in fact they WANT many of them to fail so they can step in and *privatize* education. (More about this later in the *Charter Schools Are Like Transformers* chapter!)

For now, back to our earlier question: what *does* it say when the *teachers* and *administrators* cheat on tests?

I'll tell you what it says.

It ~~says~~ *screams* that we have dropped to our knees and started worshipping the data deity (and its evil offspring of standardized tests, exit exams, and arbitrary assessments) with the kind of over-zealous fervor usually reserved for suicide bombers.

Wait, that's unfair to suicide bombers.

They only wreak havoc *once;* this ever-increasing addiction to arbitrary (and easily manipulated) numbers is going to metaphorically bomb our educational system back into the Stone Age.

Wait, that's unfair to the Stone Age, but you get the point.

So what is this cryptic thing that so many politicians and ed. reform sycophants love almost as much as the sound of their own voices? What is this Nazgul of negative effect?

da·ta—*noun; plural but singular or plural in construction, often attributive* \ dā-tə : 1. Factual information (as measurements or statistics) used as a basis for reasoning, discussion, or calculation. 2. Information output by a sensing device or organ that includes both useful and irrelevant or redundant information and must be processed to be meaningful. 3. Information in numerical form that can be digitally transmitted or processed. ("Data." *Merriam-Webster Dictionary.* Springfield, Massachusetts Web. 7 May. 2013.)

Data. The bane of modern teachers' existence, the phantom menace that has turned what used to be classroom instruction into information mining, data has become the god that administrators and curriculum "gurus" nationwide worship; and like most vengeful gods, this one requires *sacrifice*. Would you like to know *what*, exactly, is being sacrificed in this completely misguided worship of facts and figures? I'll bet you already know, but I'll confirm it for you.

The meaningful education of our children is being sacrificed.

Data. If we agree to work with the Merriam Webster definition of the word, some interesting visuals arise. *"'A sensing device or organ'… processing both useful and irrelevant or redundant information that must be processed?!?"* That's enough to conjure up images of the machines in *The Matrix* harvesting endless fields of human fetuses as batteries to power their existence. Terrifyingly, the truth isn't that far removed, it's just that the machines sit in offices and wear suits and sensible heels.

I could have written an entire book about this subject but, if you're a layman, I don't want to bore you with the details; and if you're "in education," I'd just as soon not slap the sunburn, know what I mean? For my part, I have always kept an open mind when it came to integrating education and technology, and I actually DO think that data can be useful *if the intent of gathering it is for the betterment of our children, and that it is used, punctually, consistently and logically for that end.*

But it ain't.

Ironic that my spellcheck is telling me that "ain't" ain't a real word, and suggesting I correct it. The *machine* is right, of course, but I was going for some verbal irony there, so I'll keep it, thank you. And therein we see the weak spot of compu-learning—there is no room for common sense, humor, deeper reading, or *human understanding*.

These data-driven monstrosities and their invasive databases certainly can tell each student what individual skills they need help with, and come up with 'customized' questions much faster than I could.

Robots could have probably kept much better 24/7 surveillance on my four kids when they were little, and they probably never suffered from fatigue, *but that doesn't mean I would have let them raise my children.*

I sense I'm being too vague here, so let me hit you between the eyes with some very real, and very scary, reality. Let me tell you about an article [from the June 17, 2013 TIME magazine] called *A is For Adaptive* by Kayla Webley.

NOTE: The <u>underlined stuff</u> is my doing, as I just want to draw your attention to certain lines. This is not to sway you one way or another; you can read the entire article and contact me for some spirited debate. (I'd like that.) But for now, I want you to focus on one thing in particular: WHO are the individual$ mo$t intere$ted in the$e new learning technologie$? HINT: It i$n't the kid$, the parent$ or the teacher$...

The tag line for the article is, word-for-word: *"Personalized learning is poised to transform education. Can it enrich students <u>and investors</u> at the same time?"* (Webley 40).

I speak only for myself here, but when we start worrying about appeasing investors simultaneously with educating kids; we are (at the VERY least,) splitting our priorities.

The article goes on to talk about Knewton, an educational start-up that will, according to them, create programs that "will be used to form a learning profile, a <u>sort of anonymous</u> <u>permanent record</u> <u>that travels with a student from school years though college and on to employment</u>" (Webley 42).

"Sort of anonymous?" Follow you from cradle to the grave? Hmmmm...methinks I don't like the sounds of that. Think back, honestly, to your early school experiences—Would you have wanted

YOUR "educational profile" sticking to you like that black alien thingy from Spiderman 3 for the rest of your life? People change, folks— that's why tattoo removal is big business.

Bottom line: Nobody was paying a damn bit of attention to these kinds of programs until the siren call of big money began echoing across the land. This is where you need to pay close attention, folks; because when numbers THIS big start getting tossed around, the quality of our children's education becomes waaaaaayyyyyyyyyy secondary to profit. What kind of numbers, you ask?

- Want a platform like Knewton in your school? That'll cost you between $100,000—$250,000 for a "one-time integration fee" (Webley 44).
- The global education market is, according to a variety of sources, about 5 TRILLION dollars.
- "Education-tech start-ups...attracted more than **$425 million** in venture capital **last year**" (Webley 45).

Now, to put this in perspective, let me set up a scenario and then ask you an honest question. We're friends now, so I expect an <u>honest</u> answer.

You have been offered an opportunity to invest in a company that will, by their account, create software that will quickly and accurately assess what the children [from another country that isn't yours] are good/bad at. The software will generate "personalized learning" that will be able to generate increasingly difficult questions/challenges but (because it's a computer, after all) won't be able to actually *teach* or *speak to* the children about *what* they got wrong or WHY they got it wrong. The information gathered will be—"wink-wink"— anonymous, and it will follow them for life, even later when they start looking for jobs in an already hyper-competitive economy.

(In that ultra-fast, announcer voice) *Sideeffectsmayinclude:apat*

*hy,increaseddrop-outrate,anger,frustration,andaone-dimensionalne
xtgenerationincapableofindependentthought.* Reminder: This is not
your country and the chance you'll ever encounter any of these kids
face-to-face is one in a million. Speaking of millions, you could make
enough money from this investment to ensure that you and *your* children are independently wealthy.

Do you do it?

If you answered in the affirmative, I appreciate your honesty. Take
solace in the fact that a LOT of investors share your desire to add com-
mas to the ol' bank account: According to the TIME article, "Investors
are now looking at education and saying, 'Holy cow, there's a huge
number of dollars being deployed [in educational technology.] <u>If we
can wrest free some of it, there's a huge opportunity to make money
here</u>'" (Webley 45).

Do I really need to add anything to that quote?

I thought not.

THIS is why data has become the false idol at whose altar so
many "education reformers" worship; because there is a huge opportunity to make money from it.

Ed-tech is a burgeoning business where people are trying to get
in on the ground floor the way dot-com millionaires did with the
Nasdaq back in 2000. Can't say I totally blame them; after all, a large
amount of new millionaires popped up on the radar that year ***but,***

and this is kind of important,

The PRODUCT the investors were gambling on wasn't *the human population that will determine the future of this country.*

My editor (who has become like HAL, that omnipresent, annoying
computer from 2001: A Space Odyssey) suggested that I do a quick
summary of what I've dropped on you up to this point before I continue.

Fine.

Rich people and politicians that will never *go* ANYwhere near our kids want to *test* them into one-dimensional automatons so they can measure "progress" (that they secretly don't want) in a one-size-fits-all format, sacrificing any meaningful, diversified education that might be useful in the global job market in the process. *To ensure this profoundly evil process continues* (in the face of administrators and teachers that KNOW it is counter-productive to real education) *the bastards threaten the admins and teachers with unemployment and shame if they don't* **prove** *that they have made the progress* that they are trying to prohibit in the first place, thus permanently disabling the human product: i.e—our children.

Boo-ya! HAL do you like me now? That was pretty good if I do say so myself.

Speaking of that "human product" would y'all like to know how they're *responding* to all this mining of their information resources? (I'll bet you can probably guess,) but first—another example of this disgusting data worship straight from reality.

My reality.

This year we, the members of the English department at my school, were told (not asked, *told*) that we were going to be administering YET ANOTHER computerized assessment to our students; *this* one (so we were told) would measure their reading levels and make book/story recommendations based on those levels.

Sounds pretty harmless, right?

So, in *theory*, does Socialism.

We were told (not asked, *told*) to administer this reading-level testing to our students: this **two weeks** after a *different sit-in-front-of-the-laptops-that-will-undoubtedly-freeze-because-*

of-our-crappy-bandwith-data-driven test. What was supposed to be a reading test to determine their reading levels looked, for all intents and purposes, like a vocabulary test that, upon completion, gave the kids a "Lexile Score" that confused the living daylights out of them.

Example: Natalie finished her test and was told that her Lexile score was 1,650 which, when checked against the two page(?!) scoring grid, meant that her reading level was about mid-8th grade. Considering that she was a 9th grader she was a hell of a lot closer to age-appropriate than most of the kids we tested with the "reality" of this "reading test."

I'm not gonna go into the details of how invalid this test was in testing ACTUAL reading capability, but I will share with you one specific…outcome…of this oh so helpful testing.

A colleague of mine, let's call him Josef Chipolte, had a young man finish his test, collect his Lexile score, and read to the bottom.

At first, this young man, let's call him Simba, was thrilled because he was done early and his Lexile score was a 350 (and he "knows," thanks to his nine years of public school in America, that a 100 is good, so a 350 must be super-awesome…) but then he, this 15 year-old boy,

gets to the bottom and sees the book recommendations **that the company that sponsors this particular testing software** made for him and finds, among others:

The Berenstain Bears Christmas, I'm A Big Sister, and *The Big Potty.*

Other students see this and, well, you can probably figure out the positive effect this had on this young man and how much it made him want to read, (let alone take another test like this.)

It gets better, of course. Remember that cryptic "lexile score?" Simba will eventually figure out, or be told outright, that it means he is on a mid-2nd grade reading level. But if he gets the same score next year, it will be worth *less*.

To clarify, the overall scale will change every year, with higher scores needed just to stay in the same place. THIS year Simba's 350 = grade 2.5, NEXT year the same 350 = 2.0, ostensibly keeping the students in a perpetual state of "chasing the carrot" *so they don't "get content."*

Get **content**? Ohhhhh you've no idea how hard it is to avoid profanity at times like this.

Problem: The only reason a donkey follows the carrot on the stick *is because he knows what a carrot tastes like* and *wants it again*. A BIG portion of our kids **don't know what success tastes like**, and this kind of testing does nothing but **intensify hostility, breed apathy,** and **facilitate hatred** <u>toward the teachers</u> that are forced to administer them. Yes, that's right, the KIDS (and they are justified in doing so) take their frustrations out on us, the teachers because—and you may sense a theme here—WE'RE THE ONLY ONES *AROUND* THEM WHEN THE FECES HIT THE FAN. How can a kid vent his/her hostility (about all this testing) to politicians, administrators, or venture capitalists that have NO interest *in actually being **around** the kid?!?*

Uh…they can't, so it's "shoot the messenger time" again.

Can I tell you something?

I think I speak for teachers across the country when I say that:

The messengers (teachers) are getting pretty !#@$%? tired of getting "shot" for doing dirty work *we don't believe in*, just because you administrators are trying to save your rear ends by doing what a group of clueless politicians and investors TELLS you to do!

Simply put, we see—firsthand—the damage this incessant testing is doing to the students, and being forced to play an active role in hurting the ones we love is excruciating.

This segues perfectly into the second part of my call to end the blind worship of the Data God; namely, the fact that this movement is breeding a legion of fallen angels throughout this great land of ours.

And they look an awful lot like *our children.*

No matter what tests/benchmarks/assessments/etc. are given at their school, *every* teacher can tell you how the kids *react* to them. After the initial groaning and eye-rolling, the students usually flood us with questions. I'm going to go out on a limb here and assume that, in most schools, the questions sound something like this:

- Why do we have to keep taking these tests?
- Does this affect our grades?
- Is this like/related to the test we just took?
- What happens if I just don't do this?
- Who made this test? Why? Who gets our scores? What do they do with them?
- Are we gonna have to take more of these next week? Next month? Why?
- By the way, what did we get on that last test we took? Or the one before that? Or the one before that? Or the one…

You get the point.

Legitimate questions; questions that we (the teachers that ALSO happen to hate this crap) have then passed on to the brain trust that supports said crap. The answers are usually convoluted, vague, and—in some cases—downright confrontational, bringing to mind Einstein's famous quote that *"if you can't explain it simply, you don't understand it well enough."*

You got *that* right, Mr. Theory of Relativity.

In fact, I asked one administrator, Mikel Konstantinov, point blank: "if all the kids just closed their laptops and said 'we aren't doing this' what would happen?"

He replied that "we would have to find the person who put them up to it and deal with them first" prior to giving me a look that was, I guess, supposed to inspire fear.

"Interesting;" I replied, "you don't think our kids are smart enough to know when something is counter-productive, or to speak for themselves? You willing to go on the record with **that** one Mikel?" I asked on the way out of his office.

On my way out, his secretary said, conspiratorially but plenty loud enough to be heard, "I don't think he likes you very much." To which I replied, PLENTY loud enough to be heard, "maybe someday he'll come out of his office into the *real world* and tell me that himself."

Here it is, unfiltered and unapologetic: Students across the country have had enough of this non-stop "information mining." It's bad voodoo, and they sense that. Most of the stuff masquerading as "data-driven instruction" isn't as advertised, and most of the precious data that's collected is, (by the time the idiots siphon through it and get it organized,) outdated or impertinent anyway!

Hey, we have this big ol' pile of information on Eddward; it took us all year to collect it, organize it, and [somewhat] figure out what to do with it, but we've got it!! And now you can have it!!!

Unfortunately...it's JUNE, and Eddward will be in the next grade next year and starting a whole new curriculum, with new teachers, new expectations, etc. soooooooooo *that* stuff you have there is kind of like your new cell phone—obsolete and depreciating in value by the minute. Maybe if you could have given me something to use—oh, I don't know—during the actual school year when I was *TEACHING* Eddward?

Of course, Eddward's new teacher will get this [now somewhat outdated] information on the first day of school, along with suggestions about how to personalize *every single lesson* for Edd (*and her other **140** students,*) along with the other 2 foot tall pile of paperwork (<u>not</u> kidding, <u>not</u> exaggerating, *at all*) that she will have to learn, internalize, and start implementing in the next 72 hours. I'm sure it will get her prompt attention.

NOTE: Check out Geoffrey Canada's talk on TED.com: *Our*

failing schools. Enough is enough! for some brilliant insight into the aforementioned point and, quite frankly, the whole data conundrum.

Now back to the kids—You think they don't realize that (in many schools) the only time the ones at the top of the food chain (the ones in the suits from the big offices) give a damn about them is during testing (when the scores that ultimately determine whether they keep *their* jobs are harvested?)

Teachers out there, how many of you have had your kids ask "why are the *[insert administrative titles]* in the halls today?" during state testing or something similar?

I'm sure many of you, because the kids are smarter than we give them credit for, and they know a façade when they see one. Speaking of façades—In my school, by March, certain 11th grade students have missed so many days that they are on 'non-credit status.' Guess when they get those N.C.S. letters dropped on their desks? The *day after* the state tests have been completed.

In other words—and this came, verbatim, from a student's mouth—"they got what they needed from [us] and now [we're] basically expendable."

Yes. The kids *get it.*

Remember what I said about that scene from The Matrix when the machines are harvesting fields of humans for energy to sustain their technological reign?

Yeah, something like that.

Perhaps I'm being a bit hyperbolically metaphorical, but should we even be having a discussion anywhere *close* to that when it comes to our **children**? SATs and State tests and the like are consistently referred to as "high stakes testing." High stakes? Isn't that a *gambling* term? I know I sure as hell don't want it associated with my kids.

But it is, and the anxiety, fear, discrimination and depression that this incessant wave of testing produces is unconscionable and—I'll say it—unethical. When I hear stories about little elementary school kids puking on their test booklets or young men and women having emotional breakdowns in Middle School classes, I worry that we're heading the way of China—great test scores and the highest suicide rate among students in the World.

This crap wears away at the desire of our children to *learn*…
and it anesthetizes the teachers that want to *teach*.

Oh yes, the apathetic angels I spoke of are not simply in the desks of our classrooms, many of them are standing in front of the class, and they too have grown tired of being forced to treat our kids—yes, OUR KIDS*—like automatons.

*The average high school teacher spends about 188 HOURS a year with their students, elementary teachers closer to 1,000 HOURS; of course, some put in more after school, etc. Who, I ask you (beyond close relatives) spends so much time with these children? Yes, we think of them as OUR KIDS.

I can only speak for myself—so I will.

First of all, that "lexile testing" I spoke of a little while back was about the 10th new "wrinkle" added (in 5 months?!) to an already over-worked group of English teachers. We were becoming victims of the whole "no good deed goes unpunished" thing, as we were the ONLY department in the school with consistently rising state test scores, tons of collaborative practice, etc. **The representatives from the STATE** that assessed our school said, and I quote, *"[the staff of the English Dept. of _____,] were great…and should be the model by which all other departments are judged."*

Know what our "higher ups" *heard*?

They heard: "Hey! These people seem to be the only ones around here that know what the heck they're doing, so let's put them in charge of everything we want to try because they won't screw it up.

And if they do, we can blame it on **them** *and not on our ineptitude and addiction to testing."*

I know a lot of teachers can relate.

Believe me, it takes every minute of the 10 months I have with my kids to cover the things we need to cover, and having a new "data collection test" of any kind added every couple weeks is excruciatingly time consuming for me, frustrating for the kids, and damaging to their education.

Example: **We had just begun Act II of *Romeo and Juliet*, and the newest "data-collection instrument" (surprise! Do it THIS week) took almost a full week away from us and the kids, of course, lost track of Shakespeare. We tried to pick up with a review, but that was difficult with the [mandated] State testing "concentration" coming up the following week; oh, and where is that writing sample we asked you (last week) to present, grade, and (do OUR job) record the data from?**

Think I'm kidding? I'm not—not even a little bit.

The kids start to grow frustrated, their frustration manifests itself in apathy, and we (the teachers) begin to feel helpless, and that helplessness manifests itself in…well, apathy.

But there IS an upside to all this testing and data collection! (Thank goodness…)

It gives the Superintendents and people like them pretty numbers (provided the testing goes *well*) to hold up like shiny objects to distract taxpayers and board members. Of course, the testing does NOT always go well, and *those* numbers get "filed" the same way Jimmy Hoffa got "relocated." So we keep testing (by executive order) the crap out of our kids UNTIL THEY GIVE US THE NUMBERS WE WANT TO MAKE US LOOK GOOD AND SAVE OUR JOBS, GOSH DARN IT!

That, ladies and gentlemen, is whatcha call verbal irony.

Witty sarcasm aside, I need the "educational professionals"

to give me a minute to talk to the folks *not* in the business, ok? Thanks.

Look, I know that if you're not professionally involved in education, this might have gotten a little confusing, and I'm sorry, but the simple fact is that if you pay attention to what teachers are saying—all over social media, in interviews, in private and public conversations— you'll find that the thing we complain the loudest and longest about are not, contrary to popular belief, our salaries, working conditions, or the kids.

We are sick of being told to teach your kids to pass meaningless, arbitrary, ever-changing tests that will, for the most part, have absolutely no bearing on their ability to succeed in the real world once they have left us.

We do not worship the data deity; we just want to teach your kids.

Alrighty then, I'm sure that enlightened some of you, confused a couple of you, infuriated many of you, and—at the very least—intrigued and educated a bunch of you. This section *is* called *The Road of Trials*, and I tried my best to describe the most fearsome hydra I have encountered on the road. Maybe if more people know about it, we can work together to cut all the heads off and kill this monstrosity before it devours any hope of meaningful education.

And the Cradle [of Liberty] Will Rock.

*"We're not gonna take it. No! We ain't gonna take it.
We're not gonna take it—anymore."*

—Twisted Sister

With apologies to my fellow English teachers, the aforementioned Twisted Sister lyrics, while grammatically incorrect, sound pretty good to me right about now. I was picking up some coffee at 7-11 today and the kid behind the counter (she knows me from my frequent caffeine/Gatorade runs) asked me, point blank: *"You must be pretty pissed, huh?"*

"About what?"

"The (censored) they're doing to the teachers in Philly. All your books are about that kind of (censored,) right?"

First, I told her that she was far too pretty to use language such as that...

She apologized for cursing, and thanked me for caring.

Then I thanked *her* for remembering that I wrote a few books AND even remembering *what they were about*. Now, what's all this about the teachers in my old stomping grounds of the City of Brotherly Love?

She laughed and handed me a copy of the *Philadelphia Inquirer* newspaper from behind the desk. *"A dollar fifty for the coffee, no charge for the paper; figure you can probably use this if you write another book. If you do, mention me, ok?"* she joked.

"I will" I promised.

She thought I was kidding.

I wasn't.

Thank you, Johnette.

What I read in that free newspaper made me so...***volcanically*** angry that I went straight to the gym *in my work clothes* (so my kids wouldn't suffer any residual fury that had nothing to do with them.) NOTE: As a teacher, this has happened before. Trust me; the looks you get bench pressing in dress pants and a tie are well worth *not* getting the looks from your spouse and kids when *your* stress becomes *their* stress.

And now—onto my teaching brothers and sisters in Philly and the, (as one astute young lady named Christa put it) "slap in the face...punch in the stomach, and a stab in the back, all at the same time" they were treated to.

I won't bore you with the whole story. Instead, here is a quick synopsis of the School District of Philadelphia's initial contract offer to its teachers union, early 2013 (and some color commentary from yours truly),

- **An end to the seniority-based system of filling teacher vacancies.**

    Ok, I can see that, as I have said **repeatedly** *that there are a lot of people who have overstayed their welcome in this profession, so time served should be no guarantee of being first called.*

- **An end to a guaranteed adequate supply of TEXTBOOKS and/or PAPER(?!)**

    Are you (censored) kidding me?! You want to judge my job performance (and have the right to fire me) based on my kids passing your incessant tests but I can't have **books and paper** *to teach them with?!?!*

- **No guarantees that any teacher will have a DESK.**

    But I'll bet this stipulation was created around a BIG one, with a bunch of big, fat rear-ends seated in cushy chairs around it. Oh well, at least that's one less thing the kids can throw at them, not that the teachers could do anything ABOUT it, because the district wants to...

- **Eliminate the teachers' right to use "reasonable force" to protect themselves from attack or injury.**

    Yes, you read that correctly. Please, tell me, in what profession—ANY other profession—is a person not allowed to defend themselves from attack or injury? You could look it up in the library, but...

- **Schools of all sizes would no longer be required to have *librarians* or *counselors.***

    To quote the late Ray Bradbury: "You don't have to burn books to destroy a culture, just get people to stop reading them."

- **"Steps" that give teachers higher pay for more experience and education would be *eliminated***

    *So don't bother **getting better** at your job, or **educating yourself** any further, because <u>none of it will matter</u>. In fact, with what we're [not] paying you, you'll probably have to get another job to supplement your income, (and pay for paper) which—of course—will take time away from your ability to create quality lessons.*

    Give it a minute for that to sink in and now predict what will happen to the current crop of underpaid, already overworked, teachers. Now predict what their students will look like. I'm as scared as you are.

And, for the final insult...

- **a 13 percent pay cut for those making over $55,000, and**

- **a slightly smaller cut to those making less.**

  Like the warden coming into your cell and, with guards protecting him, taking a big bite out of the cake your mother sent AS he prison rapes you. Repeatedly.

All this and more from the school district that just two years ago paid a controversial Superintendent **NINE HUNDRED THOUSAND DOLLARS** *to step down* during a climate of fiscal distress with huge layoffs of teachers and administrators. (Side note: She then <u>applied</u> <u>for</u> <u>unemployment</u>. Feel free to throw up…I almost did.)

Let me summarize this for you and, hopefully, provide just the teensiest bit of insight into why your teacher friends get a bit hostile when you tell them how *easy* they have it:

They want us to teach your kids for no money, with no supplies, and no incentive for improvement. **They** want us to improve your children's literacy with no books and no paper, and when those young men and women finally, and justifiably, snap (because even a dumb dog knows it's being abused and neglected) **they** want us to *sit back and let them assault us* while the people who are running the ship into the iceberg **get paid more, to STOP screwing things up, than** *we* (the teachers) **do in a lifetime.**

They, by the way, are the people who make the decisions we, as teachers, are forced to abide by; interestingly, <u>**"they"**</u> <u>are ever-increasingly made up of people that never did our job in ANY capacity,</u> *<u>so they are gloriously out of touch with what it takes to</u>* **<u>*do*</u>** *<u>it</u>*.

They are not unique to Philadelphia; in fact, **they** are an ever-increasing epidemic, a virus of humankind and, in the humble opinion of this author,

they deserve a slow death at the creative hands of the children whose futures they are compromising with their avarice and insensitivity.

A little follow up...

Since I wrote the previous chapter, various Philadelphia publications have published articles about the impending Doomsday Scenario facing schools in the city that bred Rocky and the Broad Street Bullies. (Good thing, too, because it's going to be one big street fight in the halls if that "budget" passes.)

One of those "we shall not go quietly" publications is *The Philadelphia Inquirer, which* has been uniquely pro-teacher and unfashionably stalwart in its exposure of educational shenanigans. According to *The Inquirer*, this is what schools in Philly will look like in September:

> No books, no paper, no clubs, no counselors, no librarian... there would be bigger classes but no aides to help manage them. Schools would lack sports, support staff to monitor lunchrooms and playgrounds, and secretaries. Some would lose security officers. Thousands of musical instruments would sit unplayed because there would be no music teachers to give lessons. Nurses, already scaled back dramatically, would be reduced to the point where one would become responsible for 1,000 students, many of whom require medication daily or are seriously ill. (Graham, Kristen A. "A doomsday scenario for Philadelphia Schools *Philadelphia Inquirer* 6 May 2013: LZ01. Print.)

Oh, and school counselors will be almost entirely cut out of most programs.

In 1909, Woodrow Wilson gave a speech to a large audience of businessmen in New York City that went something like this:

"We want one class to have a liberal education. We want another class, a very much larger class of necessity, *to forgo the privilege of a liberal education and fit themselves to perform specific manual tasks.*"

Hmmm.....

Sounds like they're finally getting around to making sure that permanent underclass of "manual task performers" gets created, doesn't it?

One school district at a time;
starting, with 1,776 tons of irony
in one of the cradles of liberty.

Charter Schools Are Like Transformers

Quick question.

How would you feel if your neighbors kept telling you that the local daycare system (that was rapidly expanding its locations and increasing the restrictions on the *types* of kids they take in) could raise your kids *better than you*, but you had a mountain of evidence that proved that the system, more often than not, sucked harder than that Noo Noo thing from the Teletubbies.

And what if you found out that the reason this new daycare system was getting so much positive press [despite so much negative outcome] was because a few of the BIG local businesses (like the local fast food franchise and the nearby cell phone dealership) were sticking their *not-so-good-for-the-kids* products in the daycares and, of course, spending wads of cash to *promote* them as a result?

You'd be pretty steamed, right?

Right.

You'd probably be hot enough to start telling people about this logistical legerdemain adversely affecting our young lads and lasses.

Too bad *nobody would listen to you.*

Yes, despite knowing what kind of job YOU do with your kids (because you CARE about them,) these daycares will **continue** to be touted as *superior to you* because a band of shady investors will continue to turn up the volume promoting them—effectively hitting the MUTE button on you and your silly "facts."

To quote the legendary Alice Cooper: "Welcome to my nightmare."

More specifically, *our* nightmare—the nightmare of frustration for the average public school teacher, who has to hear, almost daily, how virtual charter schools are becoming the solution to the "traditional education" we provide; *especially* when we know that study after study shows that these virtual schools DON'T deliver education any better than us. (Feel free to do a little research on this.)

Nonetheless, 44 states [as of the writing of this book] have been able to open virtual charter schools **using taxpayer dollars** under the argument that they are a "cost effective alternative to public education."

Cough, cough…lobbyists at work…cough, hack, cough…
Sorry.

Listen, this ain't rocket science, folks; any scholastic scenario **where profit outweighs actual student performance** is going to start generating crap very soon.

Unfortunately, as the saying goes, "crap travels downhill." The *kids* are always at the bottom of the hill, with their teachers just slightly uphill, warning them about the incoming avalanche, but unable to do anything to save them.

If, however, you still choose to "attend," or send your child to, a charter school (virtual or otherwise) let me suggest you do a bit of research first. Specifically, find out who is funding—and therefore truly RUNNING—the school in question.

Foreign investors?

Corporate money?

Disenfranchised teacher that hit the lottery?

Find out, and find out what their *agenda* is, because that will weigh VERY heavily on what will be *taught* in that school. This is actually sound advice for **any** school, but assuming that your choice of "cost effective alternative to public education" is automatically more concerned with you simply because it's…uh, alternative, is as preposterous as it sounds.

Actually, ANY scenario AT ALL where the people running (read: **funding**) the show care more about staying in the black than they do about the people they're caring for sounds like a recipe for disaster in a fast hurry. I'm sure those of you in the medical arena, military service, construction field, et.al know EXACTLY what I'm talking about…

I must confess that I'm a little too busy (ironically) "competing" against the rising red tide of charter chum to research them inten-sively beyond those in my immediate vicinity, but I can tell you this: My old stomping grounds of Philadelphia currently houses over 80 charter schools (including a few cyber charters) and about 25% of them have already been under federal or state investigation.

Your tax dollars at work.

As if that weren't laughable enough, some modern P.T Barnum decided that it would be a great idea to get kids that didn't attend regular school to enroll in ONLINE schools!

Brilliant! To quote Barnum's neighbor, David Hannum, "there's a sucker born every minute" and 6,000 of them signed their kids up to "attend" cyber-charter schools, *at a cost of* **sixty million** *dollars to tax payers who probably don't know that hardly any of them met federal academic standards…*

Just sayin'.

Don't get me wrong, people, **I'm not against Charter Schools as an idea; heck, I'm actually in FAVOR of some good old fashioned [capitalist] competition in the field of education!** However, I'm get-ting tired of hearing from parents at every soccer field, basketball court, graduation ceremony and happy hour tell me how Charter schools are the magical elixir to cure all of our academic ills.

That having been said, I encourage all parents to seek what they feel is the best course of education for their children, be it Charter School, online education, home schooling; Catholic, private, or pub-lic schooling. Just remember, do your research and stay involved in the process, because education has become, more and more, a busi-ness. A business concerned with profit over passion, cash over caring, and sometimes,

sometimes,

Charters over children.

Be careful. Very often, there is more to them than meets the eye.

PART VII
MEETING WITH THE GODDESS

At this point, our intrepid adventurer experiences a love that is all-powerful and unconditional. The meeting with the goddess (who is incarnate in every woman) is the final test of the talent of the hero to win the treasure of *love*.

She'll be mortified to be identified as "the goddess," but Dr. Shelly Ward Richards, principal of The Cleary School (along with her evil minions— John Olive and Matt Tavener) facilitated an experience that, just by its timing and altruistic nature, allowed for an epiphany that reminded this adventurer *why* he does what he does, and why he *loves* it.

Soundtrack for this chapter: *Lovely Day* —Bill Withers

It's a Buenaful Day.

An exposition, for you non-English teachers out there, is the part of the story, usually near the beginning, wherein some important background is explained. That having been explained, allow me to expose myself.

Well *that* sounded naughty didn't it?

But you love it, you know you do.

On March 17th of 2003, I was involved in a pretty bad vehicular accident. Yes, that is St. Patrick's Day and no, I had not been drinking. Actually, I was coming home from work and on my way to pick up my [then 4, 5 and 6 year-old] kids on a crystal clear afternoon. I told this story in detail in my first book so rather than be redundant, I'll simply say that my Ford F-150 was destroyed but I was not. Details aside, I am reminded every year on that day how lucky I am to be neither paralyzed nor dead.

On March 20th of 1995 my oldest son, Cain Francis Stepnowski, died from a congenital heart defect. He was 13 days old. I have three amazing kids now, who keep me too busy, and too much in love, to brood on past heartache. We also have custody of my wife's nephew, who has survived "Sparta" and become an exemplary addition to our family. Nonetheless, every year on that day I experience a profound sense of loss as I reflect on my beautiful boy, who I would have held and kissed every minute of his living days had I only known.

Needless to say, poor March 19th is under a lot of pressure every year.

Exposition taken care of, our story begins:

There I was, wedged between bookends of tragedy and reflection, when a most beautiful thing happened; a day that reaffirmed my faith in education and soothed my jaded soul, if only for a while. It would not be hyperbolic to say that my Grinchy heart grew three sizes that day.

Some time ago, my buddy and *Honey-Badger-hidden-in-the-guise-of-country-mouse-librarian*, Bridget Zino, got my books into the greedy little paws of one Matt Tavener, genuinely cool dude and appreciator of all things righteous and rebellious; then, just as Jacob begat Joseph, Matt begat John, and John begat Shelly.

Ok, nobody there really begat the others, but it sounded Bibli-cool so I ran with it.

Mr. Tavener, and his partner in crime, John Olive, forwarded my second book to some folks higher up the food chain at the Buena (pronounced byoon-ah) School District at the end of the 2011 school year, joking that "maybe this is the solution to our discipline problems."

Quick side note/shameless self-promotion: Giving my second book, *S.C.R.E.W.E.D., An Educational Fairytale* to a school administrator is like giving a cobra a box of mongooses on steroids and Red Bull.

It ain't gonna be pretty.

Or so you would *think*.

I certainly thought so.

Fast forward to late December, 2012 and the Pirates of persistence got in touch with me asking if I would be interested in visiting their school as a 'meet the author' kind of thing, and "see what hell [I] hath wrought, see what the early stages of [my] dream school *could* look like and get some props for the inspiration."

Apparently, the principal of The Cleary School, one Dr. Shelly Ward Richards *liked* the idea of holding teachers, students, and parents accountable, and was ok with me coming to her school and talking to the kids and the staff.

For my part, I thought I was being "Punked."

Once it was established that Matt and John were not, in fact, messing with my head, I accepted the invitation faster than Sonic the Hedgehog on methamphetamines.

I know...disturbing image, but I just wanted to see if I could spell methamphetamines.

We agreed that I would make the long trek to Buena Township on a day of their convenience. John stayed in touch and finally let me know *that March 19th would be a good day,* as it was a single-session day and I could meet with the kids (if I wanted to) and then speak to the staff in the afternoon.

March 19th.

Of course it is.

Fortunately, I have, at last count, about a gadgillion sick and personal days (saved up over the course of a bazillion years) so I was able to take off on that Tuesday. To be honest, I told my students that I was going to visit another school district. Technically, it was true and *that,* combined with the fact that I *never* take off, prompted rampant rumors that I was seeking employment elsewhere. I let those rumors spread and may or may not have hinted at their legitimacy.

It's nice to be wanted, and I noticed that most of my students, even the petulant little beasties with no emotional connection to anyone, seemed much more appreciative for a week or so of my "return" the following day. Any good teacher knows that if something happens that makes the kids suddenly work harder? You ride that wave until it crashes, son.

But first, I have a visit to pay, and a meeting with the goddess.

It was a misty rain 'twas falling on Tuesday, March 19th when I hopped in the Chevy Tahoe, but the weather outside was mild compared to the storm that was brewing inside yours truly. Oh yeah, a freakin' mess I was, worse than a teenage girl.

What should I wear? Don't want to look too pretentious, but I don't want these people to think I don't take them seriously, *she used my book as inspiration for cryin' out loud?!* Get there early? Yes. Always arrive early—for everything—on time is too late for great men, right? Think you're great, then Step? Feeling a bit more pompous than usual today, are we? Shut up. Should I take autographed books or offer to sign theirs? What make you think they want your autograph? Dear LORD you are a self-important twat…

(NOTE: This is but a sample of the arguments waged in my head. I know, it's a small miracle I get anything done at all.)

White dress shirt, untucked, black suit jacket, nice jeans, black Chuck Taylors; classy but informal. Take signed copies for the spouses. Leave early, allow time for getting lost and get there with plenty of time for introductions and directions.

(Yeah, yeah…in addition to hearing voices, I am directionally challenged—without GPS, I couldn't find my way home from across the street,)

I'll spare you all the self-congratulatory nonsense and get right to it. I arrived around 11:30 and was graciously welcomed by John, who introduced me to *everyone*, including the teachers, all of whom, without prompting, felt compelled to tell me how much they loved working there, and how the fact that the administration working *with* them and consulting *with* them has helped transform the school into what it is today.

NOTE to administrators that hide in their offices and make demands from a comfortable distance: There might be a message in there somewhere.

Whoops! Almost allowed my bitter herbs to sour this sweet experience; back to the day at hand: I made my way down the halls, stopping when I could to talk to the kids, who were direct and inquisitive, funny and brazen—the way most kids are until we teach them to sit, down, shut up, and do what the adult in the room says.

Oops, I did it again.

I was invited to sit in on Matt's science class and then, time permitting, the kids would be allowed to ask a "real author" questions. I would then do the same in John's class, and finish the afternoon by speaking to the staff.

I sat down at Matt's desk, in the back of the room, and took a look around. He had, with the creative use of aluminum foil, turned his entire back wall into a "refrigerator door" where all the kids' great work could be hung. Genius. I then immediately noticed a few things around Matt's desk: His Star Wars lunch box, a quote from Henry Rollins hanging on his bulletin board, student papers with a LOT of notes written on them, and my books (with pages folded and Post-it notes stuck inside) on his desk. Oh yeah, me and this guy are gonna get along *very* well…

Watching his class of 5th graders learn about mineral properties (by "disassembling" M&M cookies,) I was reminded of the desire to learn that kids come to school with (again—before we strangle it out of them) and their fearlessness in both asking questions and volunteering answers. I vowed to myself to try to rekindle that in some of my more reticent students when I got home. In the meantime, it was Q&A with the 10 year-olds!

Honestly, I thought I would be like Beck Bennet in those AT&T commercials—you know, the ones with the guy sitting in a classroom with the little kids: *"What's better, fast or slow?"* but I was very pleasantly surprised at the full frontal assault launched by those little buggers.

First three questions:

"Do you feel any pressure to make your book really good now that people liked your first two?"

"Do you hate some of the stuff you write? 'Cause I hate some of the stuff I write?"

"How much money do you make writing books?"

Wow.

Those are some pretty good questions.

I answered, we talked, we laughed and we learned—ALL of us learned. I could've gone all day but it was time to visit another class.

Oh, and the kid who "hated the stuff he wrote?" Apparently, he is a hell of a writer, but never submitted *anything* because he didn't think anyone else would like it. After I talked to him, I am very proud to say that he started submitting more work. I made a mental note to ask my high school students how many of them felt that way and what, if anything, changed them.

On to an English class, and another burst of inspiration, and another round of intriguing, politically incorrect questions. I was in heaven. I felt the same way as I do when I visit other teachers' classes at my own school but even more so because I was really out of my element (and area code!)

After some pictures with Matt, John, and Dr. Richards, it was time to talk to the staff. It should be noted that Shelly (Richards) was very cool—she posed for a picture with her "scolding" me in the principal's office (ah, memories!) and, if I may be honest, is far too cute to be a principal. If getting sent to *her* office was a punishment, I would have been an ever more mischievous little bast…

But I digress.

I was honored, and a bit anxious, to speak in front of my peers. Many of them had read the books, some hadn't, ALL of them had come, voluntarily, to listen to some half-assed teacher who fancied himself an author (instead of taking that precious time to work on their stuff.) They seemed willing to let me shoot from the hip for a while, but then I mentioned that the second book was a catharsis of sorts to try and work through my frustration with the nonsense that made it so hard to teach these da…

"How do you deal with it? The nonsense. How?"

That question came in a voice that was cracking with emotion; from a woman who seemed to ask that question from somewhere deep, in a place that seemed very uncertain about whether to keep teaching. Judging from her age (she seemed at least my age) I ascertained that this was a teacher being beaten down by our anti-teacher policies in anti-teacher America. When I addressed her directly I saw tears in her eyes that she, proudly and to her credit, refused to let fall. I also saw other teachers comforting her, and the ones that weren't seemed *very* interested in my answer, as did Dr. Richards.

So, gentle but attentive reader, what did I do?

What do I *always* do when the heat is on?

Correct. I tell the truth.

I told her that "I don't worry about the new rules, restrictions, testing procedures, lesson plan formats, teacher evaluations, etc. etc. because the people who keep changing everything:

A) Have *no idea* what the hell they're doing
B) Never leave the safety of their offices long enough to come around and see if we're *doing* their changes du jour, and even if they did,
C) they would see that you're a great teacher, that the kids were actively engaged, behaving well and learning, and by the time they realized which of their new toys you weren't playing with, they'll have read something new and bought new ones. Screw 'em. YOU know what's best for your kids, you DO what's best for your kids," (at this point I saw that the tears were starting to win so it was time to shut up) and "that teaching will always, *always* boil down to whether you care or not, if you do, you'll find a way to deal with everything and your kids will follow your lead."

In my fervor to empower this woman, who was obviously a good teacher in a bad way, I forgot that my words may have been construed as reflecting negatively on "the boss," so I cautiously glanced over to Dr. Shelly Richards, who was smiling, applauding quietly, and nodding approvingly.

An administrator who loves her staff, embraces the truth, and inspires her students?

Meeting with the Goddess indeed.

I left Buena School District with two new friends in Matt and John, a ton of ideas to implement in my classroom, a new sense of self-awareness, a reminder that our students (no matter their age) are just kids, and a renewed sense of purpose in writing this book. The good teachers need to know they're not alone, and that they're doing a great job in spite of a rising tide of…well, you know.

I love being a teacher, for so many reasons, and my "Meeting with the Goddess" was a beautiful (or should I say Buenaful?) reminder of that.

PART VIII
TEMPTATION

During the course of any adventure, the hero will encounter temptation (in any variety of forms) designed to lead him astray from his/her quest.

While there is no shortage of *physical* temptation within the teachers' lounges of the world (there are some pretty hot physical specimens in front of the classrooms of America,) that's not the kind of temptation that winked and smiled at me on this particular journey.

Nor was it temptation of a *financial* nature, (I'm a *teacher* and _self-published_ author, so when I ask the "Magic 8-Ball" if piles of money are in my future it actually **laughs** at me.)

No, gentle reader, the temptation that rubbed my weary shoulders and whispered in my ear was the oldest, and most insidious of enemies—fear.

Soundtrack for the chapter: *It's a secret, but you'll know soon enough…*

Rosa Is Right.

Rosa Louise McCauley Parks was, among so many other things, pretty darn intelligent. Knowing a little something about bravery in the face of adversity, she affirmed that she had *"learned over the years that when one's mind is made up, this diminishes fear; knowing what must be done does away with fear."*

Sometimes, old friends come to visit just when you need them the most.

Sometimes their timing is quite the opposite.

Some of my old friends arrived, en masse, when I had this book more than three quarters finished, and had already told the whole damn world to expect it by Summer's end.

Enter fear, self-doubt, the absolute certainty that what you're doing is pathetic and useless, the "protective" inner voice that whispers, compassionately, that *nobody cares what you say, and you're only going to get yourself in trouble for a bunch of people that will turn their backs on you when things get* unpleasant...

The self-destructive inner drill sergeant that interrogates, loudly, *"who the hell do you think you are claiming to speak for an entire **profession**? You are a self-important ass with an ego the size of the Mt. Fuji!"*

...*"And what about your **job**?"* snickered the 'job security' voice, "sure you want to rock the boat like that?"

So *many* of my old friends showed up for the party, and they had so *much* to say.

I can't claim to know what a full blown panic attack feels like but I'm pretty sure I had one when all of the voices started talking at once. I actually said, out loud, to nobody in particular—"I could just scrap this whole project, and nobody would care, nobody would know."

Screeeeeeeeeeeeeeeeeeeeeeeeeeeeeeeeeeeeewwwwwwww **THAT.**

To paraphrase the elegant, Ms. Parks: "This book HAD to be written, and knowing that erases all fear."

If *one person* cares, that is enough

If my ego allows me to speak for those who would remain silent, then I embrace it.

I keep my job because I'm really, **really** good at what I do, not because I'm *compliant.*

So for all the voices (real and imagined) that would just as soon I stay quiet. I've got a song for you; call it the soundtrack for this chapter.

Look up the band <u>Rage Against the Machine</u>, now find the song *Killing in the Name*, crank it up LOUD, fast forward to *4:13*, and let the song play out.

That's for you, fear.

PART IX
ATONEMENT WITH THE FATHER

In this step, the person must confront, and be initiated by, whatever holds the ultimate power in his life. In many myths and stories this is a father figure, who holds the power of life and death.

This will be a short chapter, for reasons that will soon be self-evident. I will tell you this, though: this chapter contains the most painful sentence I have ever written on paper.

Soundtrack for this chapter: *Hurt* —Johnny Cash

The Fallen

When my parents divorced in 1985 I was a very angry, very impressionable young man. I vowed (angry and upset at the loss of the only stability I ever knew or needed,) to create myself in my own image and that I would never *ever* answer to anyone again.

Pulling the scab off of that memory now, as a 45 year-old man, I am impressed by two things: One, what a magnificently arrogant, albeit completely naïve little prick I was. And two, how long I actually managed to hold onto that self-destructive and isolationist mindset.

Right up to March 20th, 1995.

As I mentioned earlier, my son Cain died on that date, and I made a new vow, one born out of a pain that—compared to my parents' divorce—was like rolling around on the surface of the Sun versus a minor sunburn. I promised him that I would live with *relentless* intensity, living the life he was deprived of AND the one I was given; two lives squeezed into one—my promise.

And I did. For almost **18 YEARS** I lived like Death was right behind me in an all-out sprint, fingertips mere centimeters away. I slept less than any normal human should, pushed my body past its reasonable limits, all while (Take a deep breath:)

- Changing jobs, (from teaching hardcore special ed. to over 120 students a year.)
- Having my wife change jobs (which led to her being home less and less.
- Having my in-laws move in with us, (not as bad as you might think.)
- Renovating TWO houses (kill me now, please.)
- Seeing my brother-in-law's house burn down (and have him live with us,)
- Having another brother-in-law live with us, and ultimately die from the drug abuse that made his living with us almost tear apart my family.
- Seeing my only sibling divorce and relocate.
- Co-owning a restaurant/bar from May—October (*in addition* to teaching.)
- Earning my Masters (and seeing Dawn earn her Doctorate in Nursing practice.)
- Taking legal custody of the special needs 7 yr.-old son of the deceased brother-in-law.
- Writing, editing, promoting and self-publishing two books.
- Enduring the usual slings and arrows that having a life happily provide

>Oh, and the little matter of **RAISING THREE CHILDREN ...** (which would have been *more* than enough, believe me.)

I didn't care; I *parented* like the fate of the world hung on every decision, *taught* like I parented, *exercised* like I had signed a contract, *worked* like I was the TWO best employees at every job I took, and *husbanded* (is that a word? It should be.) like Dawn was threatening to leave me every other minute.

...sadly, ironically, *pathetically*, she probably was;

because, in doing all of the aforementioned and more, I hurt a lot of people that I perceived (in my hyper-driven haze) as lazy, uninspired, or irrelevant.

Worse, *I did so while insulating myself from harm in the "knowledge" that I was fulfilling a promise to a deceased boy who probably would have, given the chance, told me just to be happy and **enjoy** his mom, his brothers and sisters, and the people and places in my life.*

You cannot imagine how bad it hurt to write that last paragraph. You cannot imagine. But there it is.

I want to just stop here, but a lesson was learned, and if there is to be *any* good come from my near two decades of self-flagellation, maybe I can help *you* avoid the pain that comes from allowing your misplaced drive to run roughshod over your heart.

To be a really good teacher, you have to adopt an almost monastic devotion to your craft, and that very often takes a terrible toll on you and those you love.

The *bitterness* leaks into your family life—snapping at your wife for taking [an important] phone call from work in the middle of "date-night" because you're so fed up with kids checking their cell phones when you're trying to teach, damn it!

The *exhaustion* almost always causes you to shortchange the people you *don't* get paid to help—getting far too quickly frustrated when helping your son with his research paper because you've already done this fifty times today, for Christ's sake!

The PTSD-like symptoms force you to overreact to otherwise minor events at home. You "go off," saying things you wish you could say at work, yelling (with far too much stored-up disdain in your voice) at your own children about how "this is just another example of how you kids can't follow simple directions! You want everything done for you but God forbid you do anything for me!"

…or something like that. Of course, it's not your spouse or your kids you're yelling at, is it?

No, it isn't.

But, as so very often happens in the lives of those of us who put everything we've got into teaching…

we only hurt the ones we love.

I hurt the ones I love, a lot. I internalized that, a lot.

It became too much.

Medical issues, psychological issues, family issues, work issues, issue issues.

One cannot drive a truck like a NASCAR vehicle for almost 20 years without the wheels coming off and the engine blowing up, and somewhere around the Spring of 2013—

Frankie went boom.

So I went to visit Cain.

This will come as a revelation to everyone I know, as I have never told a soul until this moment. I also swore that I would never visit his grave because my son was a little boy, a perfect little boy and that was how I was going to remember him, not as some hole in the ground. But I needed him, and I needed the clarity that being near— that place—might give me.

I asked him to forgive me, because I couldn't do it anymore.

My students were suffering.

His mom, my wife, was suffering.

His brothers and sisters were suffering.

All because I was trying to do too much, *and I was starting to hate everything and everyone in the process.*

I got it all out, and I gripped that little patch of Earth like I was holding the planet in place. Grass may not grow there for a long, long time.

Doesn't matter, because I'm never going back.

I don't know if Cain forgave me, I don't know if I needed forgiveness, I don't know if I deserved forgiveness, I don't know what the hell I deserve, but I know that I'm living one life now, and the newly found room to breathe is exhausted only in trying to *enjoy* what I do.

Even raising teenagers.

Even *teaching* teenagers.

And speaking of that...

PART X
APOTHEOSIS

This is a difficult stage to define, so let's keep
it simple; this is where the hero "dies" (literally
or metaphorically) in order to move beyond the
constraints of this world so he can achieve a state of
divine knowledge.

Obviously, I didn't die (much to the chagrin of *some* people,) but I
did have, in the midst of terrible frustration a "moment of clarity" and
self-awareness that left me feeling, for the first time—in many, many
moons—pretty damn good about myself. More importantly, I felt
emboldened (from the reaction of my peers) to try to put their fears to rest
and empower them in the face of [what they perceived to be] a coming
storm. I truly, TRULY hope many more of you find comfort in these words
because you, too, are Hall of Famers in your field,
I know you are.

Soundtrack for this chapter: *Better Than You* —Metallica

I *Am* Michael Jordan
(The Danielson Model and Me)

OK, so there I was, in the back room of the school library, trying frantically to create a rubric for the class I would be teaching in
25 minutes, because they had a project due on Thursday and I was
delusional enough to believe (having put a LOT of time into making
the project creative and suited to each student's individuality,) that
they might work on it over the weekend, and I wanted them to have
specific, easy to understand, directions that would further clarify the
specific, easy to understand, directions I had already given them.

I had twenty minutes to create the rubric, print it out, run 50 yards
down the hallway (hoping not to encounter students fighting, loiter-
ing, yelling, engaging in foreplay, or a fellow staff member needing
assistance)* to the front office, beg Ms. Joyce to make me 50 copies,
and arrive to class looking like I had this done a week ago and get
rocking right into today's meticulously planned lesson.

***Chances of NOT encountering one or more of the aforementioned
roadblocks: roughly the same odds as me swimming through a nautical
mile of chum off South Africa with no shark sightings.**

Miraculously, praise Allah, I *did* manage to get all of that done and hand off the still warm rubrics to my appreciative students, who pointed out that I had *already* given them directions (which many of them misplaced) but that these NEW directions (which many of them would ignore) would, actually, help.

You can't say I didn't try, folks; especially since I did all that whilst engaging in two conversations that, while brief, helped me overcome my self-loathing for a while.

As I was frantically typing away, one of my more vocal comrades-in-arm, let's call him Stefan' Wally, plopped down next to me and began, as is his wont, to begin [in the middle of the story] to talk *animatedly* about his feelings on the subject. It was now my job to dissect my brain in two, engaging Wally in conversation while completing the *now-even-more-rushed-yet-soon-to-be-ignored* rubric.

"Ok, so my question is," began my nattily clad companion, "how are they gonna determine what percentage of the Danielson model is dedicated to extracurricular activities?"

To which I replied: *"Huh?"*

"The Danielson model, the newest 'system' by which we will be evaluated as teachers, they have to figure out how…"

"Heard enough," I interrupted, *"don't (expletive) care."*

Wally laughed, and he knows me well enough to know I wasn't kidding. Nonetheless, I was intrigued now (damn him) and my Esquire reading friend was, no doubt, better versed in this new controversy than I was, so…

"Alright Wally, you've got 5 minutes, explain this (expletive) to me in clear, concise terms, and do it while I finish this rubric.

Stefan', bless his metrosexual heart, didn't miss a beat: "OK, so you know that New Jersey is jumping all over this new model for teacher evaluation, right?"

"Right."

"And it was 'created' ("quote sign" thingies made in the air with fingers) by Charlotte Danielson who, herself, said it was never intended to be…"

"*Irrelevant*" I interrupted (again) "*stick to **what** it is, **how** it affects us, and **why** people are losing their (expletive) minds about it.*"

Wally, undaunted, did as he was told: "OK, as teachers, we used to be evaluated about 90% on what we did in the classroom…"

"*As opposed to?*"

"…but now that's only, like 45% of the evaluation model."

"Percentages and arbitrary language, this is already a (compound expletive;) but please continue."

"Another 10% or so is based on test scores, and another percent will be based on what you do outside the classroom, like coaching and moderating clubs, but they haven't figured out what percentage of the 'evaluatory pie chart' (quote signs in the air again) that this will encompass, but once this is plugged into the algorithm…"

"*Stop.*"

"Wally couldn't help but laugh at my interruption. In fact, I think he was enjoying provoking the reaction he knew he was going to get. Truth be told, he was really laughing at the absurdity of the "evaluation model" upon which he was elaborating. I had a million questions, comments and expletives for him but, as I might have mentioned, I was in a hurry, so I provided him (and a certain third party that was eavesdropping) with a concise synopsis of my feelings:

"*Heard enough; don't (expletive) care.*"

Rubric freshly printed via the library printer, I was off to sprint though the chum off South Africa, I bid Wally a fond adieu, apologizing (sincerely) for my curt behavior and asking (hopefully) if we could speak more on this later when we both had (sarcastically) some "free time."

NOTE: Much as I pick on him, co-workers like Stefan' Wally are invaluable resources. They, the dirt-digging, internet scouring, gossip

filtering minority, have the energy and gumption to become well-versed on the stuff those of us in need of a 25th hour just don't have the time to research. Cultivate these people, they can give you the 411 on (expletive) like the Danielson model in five minutes while you listen with one ear and type with two hands, and that is nothing to sneeze at.

Off I went, and just as I was about to exit the library like a defensive lineman starting the 40-yd. dash at the combine...

"Hey, Mr. Step...Step, hey, do you have a quick second?"

Slowly I turned...step by step...inch by inch... half out the door in spirit, bringing me face to face with a certain marionette whose string pullers had, not two days prior, danced him into presenting a Powerpoint on the Danielson model that was, to put it mildly, a (expletive) train wreck—mainly because the puppet—let's call him Keyser Soze—was trying to speak like an expert on something that was still in the embryonic process of being implemented. He had "inadvertently" overheard me and Wally, and was feeling froggy, so he jumped:

"I couldn't help but hear part of your dialogue about the Danielson model, and I have to say, and please don't take offense, that I am disappointed, no, not disappointed, wrong choice of word, I am...curious? Yes! Curious, as to why you..."

"Don't (expletive) care?" I interrupted.

"Yes," he admitted, looking both offended at my choice of words and relieved that *he* didn't have to say it, *"I was...curious as to why, because if you look closely at the Danielson model..."*

"I hate to cut you off, Keyser (not true) *but I have a class to teach,* (true) *so let me make this quick and simple..."*

And it was at this moment, gentle reader, that I had an epiphany. <u>A sudden and striking realization came upon me;</u> one that might never have arrived had I not achieved the apex of frustration, but one which I pass on to every single good teacher out there because, in this regard, you are all just like me, and we are ALL "like Mike:"

"I don't (expletive) care because I'm Michael (expletive) Jordan. How do you wanna measure greatness? Professional performance-like championship rings or playoff appearances? How about individual accolades-like MVPs or scoring titles? How about quantifiable im-provement over time? Maybe intangibles—like heart, tenacity and leadership? Whatever criteria you use, it doesn't faze me, because I'm good, I know I'm good, and even if the evaluation model changes, I'll still be fine BECAUSE I CONSIDER IT MY JOB TO BE GOOD AT EVERYTHING.

Michael Jordan.

Me.

Got it?

Good. So now you understand why I'm not worried about the Danielson model or whatever the (expletive) flavor of the year will be next *year. Now, if you'll excuse me I have to, ironically,* **go teach.***"*

Two of my fellow teachers and one library assistant overheard that conversation and they still laugh about it, occasionally referring to me as "Michael" in hushed, private-joke-type voices.

The truth is, my self-congratulatory paroxysm of professional pon-tificating was just a frustrated response to the winds of change that are constantly blowing in the face of me and all of my brothers and sisters in the education field.

Listen, folks, I am certainly not Michael Jordan,

(although I **will** *drain that soft kiss off the backboard from the top of the key in your face if you don't play tenacious D,)*

but I do feel like my passion for my job, and the subsequent dedi-cation that comes as a result , makes me immune to the changing winds of evaluation, which invariably smell like we're downwind from a field of bulls.

You're not Michael Jordan, either,*

*Unless you are, in which case, "Hey Mike, thanks for reading; love the Hanes undershirts."

but your commitment to your students, and the soul-sucking amount of work you put in to doing right by them, make you *like* Mike. There will always be winds of change swirling about; if your wings are tipped properly, those winds will only elevate you, and if they are tipped downward, you will be forced low and grounded. So hold your head up, keep doing what you do, and trust in the fact that you're good *because* you care.*

*Unless you DON'T care (and there are a lot of you ;) in which case, you suck and you *should* be grounded.

Epilogue: "What the Heck is a Danielson Model?"

I know that, for some crazy reason, non-teachers actually read my books, too (Hi, Mom) so I thought perhaps a quick, unbiased explanation of this thing might be in order:

According to an early 2013 *New York Times* article, "the Danielson model emphasizes four areas in terms of teacher evaluations:

1. The quality of questions and discussion techniques
2. a knowledge of students' special needs
3. the expectations set for learning and achievement, and
4. the teacher's involvement in professional development activities.

The section for assessing the strength of the classroom-learning environment has **15** criteria *down to the placement of furniture.*

The method also contains training for administrators on how to carry out the evaluations," (uh oh...) "and is designed to provide meaningful feedback on how teachers can improve and correct any issues it identifies."

As of the writing of this book, about 30% of New Jersey schools were using the model, but the rash is spreading, and the scary part is that EVERY person I interviewed, when asked *why* it was so great, gave me some version of *"well, at least everybody is doing the same thing now, and <u>uniformity</u> is the key to success."*

Really?

Interesting.

Because I'm pretty sure John F. Kennedy had it right when he said that "the unity of freedom has never relied on uniformity of opinion."

Just sayin'.

In the meantime, methods of "teacher evaluation" will come and they will go. None of them will be more critical of you than you are of yourself.

I know.

So, if you're one of those *good* teachers, the kind that beats yourself up worrying about whether you'll survive the next wave of "instructional assessment," this is from me to you:

Listen, you probably know this already, but my testosterone-driven self-promotion and profane sermonizing are but a hyperbolic façade designed to cover a person almost entire at war with himself.

Again, I'm pretty sure I'm not alone in this.

Just about every teacher, aide, substitute or counselor I know that's worth a damn can, at day's end, tell you everything they did *wrong* **in excruciating detail.**

But ask them to tell you what they did *right* and you'll get a laundry list of *"well **this** went well, but if I did it again I would…"* or *"**that** was pretty effective, but I already thought of a way to make it better if I could just…"*

Does that sound about right? If it does, take heart, and…
(with apologies to Rogers and Hammerstein:)

Walk on through the wind,
Walk on through the rain,
Tho' your dreams be tossed and blown.
Walk on, walk on
With hope in your heart
And you'll never walk alone.

—*Step*

PART XI
THE ULTIMATE BOON

The Ultimate Boon is the "big [material] payoff,"—
you know, the prize that the hero *thought* he was
after, the accomplishment of the quest that he
thought was the endgame. (We all know that self-
knowledge is the ULTIMATE reward, and the freedom
to live self-aware is the TRUE endgame, but more
on that later.) In the meantime, let's throw our well-
intentioned adventurer a bone to keep him going.

It was a beautiful night for a baseball game…

Soundtrack for this chapter: *Centerfield* —John Fogerty

15 Minutes Is Enough

Friday, May 11th, 2012, 2:30 pm. Work is done, the usual check list of chores and kids' games/practices loom on the horizon, along with the mountains of papers to mark and things to do…

But all that will be put on hold tonight.

Perfect weather on the horizon; it's a beautiful night for baseball.

Specifically, it's a beautiful night in every conceivable way, because I am being honored at the start of tonight's Philadelphia Phillies game, in front of 44,000 fans (and untold legions watching at home) *for being a good teacher.*

But it gets better. My wife, my children, my parents, and my in-laws will all be in attendance; they will share in my unbridled joy and maybe—hopefully—be proud of me.

But it gets better. My fellow teachers have shown up in force to raise their plastic cups in salute. Among them some of my dearest friends, among them not one microbe of jealousy, resentment, or bitterness; nothing but the unbridled joy that comes from seeing good teachers get the spotlight, if only for a few minutes, that every one of them deserve.

NOTE: I know how they feel. I sat where they are sitting tonight last year—and watched my friend and teaching phenom, Joshua

Kates, receive the same award, presented to him by Ed Trautz, another one of ours and as good a teacher as ever walked the planet. I was so happy for them; as I screamed along with the other teachers (we support our own 'round here) I actually got goose bumps. I couldn't believe that anyone up in all of those seats might have felt that way about me.

But it gets better. A lot better. *All* of this: the newspaper coverage, the VIP dinner before the game, the tour of the locker rooms, the signed swag, the face on the Jumbotron, the award itself, given *on the field...* all of this is the product of one young lady,

a student

my student,

a young lady that I pushed to be better than she allowed herself to be.

A young lady that, while she didn't always *like* me, understood (like one of my own children) that everything I did was to make her better.

Tanisha Crawford.

Tanisha, the year after she had me as a student, wrote a 500 word essay about yours truly, sent it to the Phillies organization, and it was one of ten chosen from *thousands* of submissions. And so, one day:

"Hey Step!"

"Hello Tanisha, how are you my dear?"

"Did the Phillies contact you?"

"I don't think they're that desperate yet, kiddo."

"No" she was bubbling over with excitement, *"about the teacher award night..."*

I would be lying if I told you I remember the whole conversation after that. I know that Tanisha left, beaming and saying *"see you at the game!"* and I know that it didn't fully sink in until, literally minutes later, my cell phone rang and it was a representative from the Phillies organization. Everything was a blur, but I knew Trautz could fill me in on the details (after the previous year's celebration) so I just went along, thanked the rep. and hung up.

And then I cried. Quiet, dignified tears, you bastards, not teenage girl watching *The Notebook* tears. Ok, there might have been a sniffle or two I don't remember… I thought "My wife will get to see this, my parents will get to see this, my kids… (more *quiet, extremely dignified* tears) Alright, get yourself together you big #@!%$ sissy…"

"What's up with you, Step? Allergies?" asked one of the girls in my next class, for which I was late, and I am *never* late.

*"Were you **crying**?"* inquired one of the 11th grade boys in the front.

"Yes, I was."

Well THAT hit the mute button on the room, so I told them what was going on, and every single one of them smiled—big, legitimately happy, NOT fake-I'm-pretending-to-be-happy-for-you smiles, and they clapped, and they came up and shook my hands and hugged me and stuff. They were happy for me. How do you like that?

But it gets better.

The night of the game, Dawn and I met up with the teachers in the parking lot of Citizen's park for some tailgating and ball busting. I was told that I would be offered the chance to dance with the (Phillies mascot) Phanatic on the dugout and that none of them would ever cover a class for me again if I opted out of the 7th inning stretch production of *A Chorus Line*.

Damn Kates and his inside knowledge…

Then Dawn and I met up with Tanisha and her mom and little brother in the VIP tent, where we were treated to dinner and treats and swag. It was her first ever baseball game, and Tanisha could barely contain her excitement, which made ME even more excited. I decided to let go of any semblance of the tough guy routine and walked around smiling like Charlie in the freakin' Chocolate Factory for the next few hours. When the food was done being served, Tanisha and I were escorted to the locker rooms and press areas for pictures, a tour, and the rundown of the proceedings. Then we walked out onto the field, where our names were announced over the PA, each nominator read their letter, and then presented the award to the nominee.

When Tanisha read her letter, I swear to you, *I had an out of body experience*. When I got the award, and we pointed to the section where our friends and families were, and heard that dull roar of joy and approval, well…

Deep, **life-changing**, vindication right there, people.

We were then reunited with Dawn and Tanisha's mom in the "Teacher All—Star seats" to watch the game. I kept looking at my wife and Tanisha. Dawn seemed legitimately happy that I was happy and, after all we've been through, her smile on that night is burned into my memory. And Tanisha, for all the torture I put that kid through, sitting there laughing and being the *real* All Star of the evening…

Perfect.

But it gets better, and I don't care if you're tired of hearing that, it was awesome and I'm going to **tell** you about it.

This is *The Ultimate Boon* chapter, after all…

Our cell phones started going crazy. Apparently, the awards were being broadcast on TV during a commercial break and the announcers were going off about how "no student would mess with the guy in the Captain America shirt" and made reference to the size of my arms.

Not gonna lie, folks, when you're an old fart with an ego that would make Gene Simmons blush and major-league anxiety about loss of "coolness"—there are worse things that could happen.

My 15 minutes of fame, right?

I have since been told that students from the last 25 years, across the Tri—State area jumped off their couches or pointed at TVs in bars and screamed some variety of "Holy (expletive) that's my teacher on TV!!"

Still "their teacher."

Nice .

Alright, I've bored you to death and talked far too much about myself here **but I have to say this to everyone out there working your soul to smithereens thinking that the most recognition you'll ever get is a pat on the back and a watch when you retire—**

Two weeks from today will mark the one year anniversary of that night, but as I wrote this, a few *extremely quiet, extremely dignified* tears formed and a big, still-in-the-Chocolate-Factory smile was etched across my otherwise unattractive countenance.

Because it happened, from the perfect source, on the perfect night, in front of the perfect people, I got my "15 minutes of fame,"and it was enough.

And yours will be, too, I promise.

Of course, the real star of that evening was Tanisha, who gave me so many things that evening. Check me out on Facebook, look for the "Teacher of the Year Night" pictures: I'm the big idiot in the Captain America shirt, she's the beautiful young lady in the Phillies shirt next to me. The "award" I received that night was the letter, framed and such, preserved so that I could read it, again and again, to remind me why I do what I do the way that I do it.

Like everything else about that evening, Perfect.

With her kind permission, I have included the letter that led to that fateful night.

It is, indeed, The Ultimate reward.

There is no way to compliment someone as great as my teacher in 500 words or less. However, I am going to try. Everyone has talked about that one teacher who you will always remember, no matter how old you get. I have already met him. I remember walking into Step's classroom in the beginning of 9th grade, taking one look at him, and thinking, "I must be in the wrong class!" No one would ever guess that Step was a literature teacher. Standing 6ft 4in tall, and weighing over 260 pounds, he looked as if he should be working as a bodyguard instead of a teacher, fending off 10 guys at once, with one hand tied behind his back. (I wouldn't hold it against him either).

Reading that, one wouldn't think that he would "allow every child to feel safe and loved" but let me tell you, unintentionally, Step became more like a guidance counselor. Actually he became more like a father, because personally, I told him things I was even too afraid to tell my parents. He always told us never to say we *couldn't*, because our minds are way more powerful than we think.

Step also taught us to have respect for ourselves, before we respected anyone else. Going to his class always felt more like a privilege than a task. During his class, he would always have us laughing until we cried, but somehow, we always got done what was required, and even more. Step always took the opportunity to teach us things that did not have anything to do with Language Arts. One day it would be about his adventures and mishaps teaching at his old school, the next day it would be about the wars that are taking place overseas. I can honestly say that I have learned as much from him in one year than I would from any other teacher in many years.

During the year of 2011, Step was diagnosed with a heart condition. If we hadn't seen the heart monitor, I don't think Step would have mentioned it. He is just that type of person, that no matter how bad he is hurting, he will continue on, as if nothing is wrong. He is still teaching, a year later, which shows how strong his heart really is. It's crazy how the people who make the biggest impact on our lives are the ones who carry the biggest burdens. Even if I don't win this contest, I want Step to know that (at least to one of his many students) what a huge phenomenon he is. I also want to thank him, for showing me who I want to be, and never, ever giving up on me, even when I gave up on myself.

—Tanisha Crawford

PART XII
REFUSAL OF THE RETURN

"The adventurer must eventually return… and [the hero must] begin the labor of bringing the runes of wisdom…into the kingdom of humanity. But the responsibility has been frequently refused."
(Joseph Campbell *The Hero With A Thousand Faces*.)

What could possibly prevent me from unleashing book 3 (my personal "runes of wisdom") upon the public? How about *Stress-Induced Susceptibility to Sudden Cardiac Death?*

Soundtrack for this chapter: *Life'll Kill Ya* —Warren Zevon

You're Killing Me
(quite literally).

Before we begin here, let me set the record straight. I am not a doctor, nor do I play one on TV, so my medical knowledge is limited at best. My wife is a doctor, but when I plugged her for information (insert you own "let's play Doctor" joke here) I realized that she is physically incapable of giving answers that would be easily understood by the reading public. So I'm going to keep the medical stuff simple and the tone humorous.

This in no way diminishes the importance of this chapter.

I am pretty damn sure that if you're a teacher, or if you know anybody in the profession, that you or someone you know is suffering very serious health issues DIRECTLY RELATED to the stress that comes from the ever-increasing, and ever-intensifying, demands of our profession. I certainly do, and it made me wonder if I wanted to add onto that stress by publishing a book sure to cause controversy. Of course, you're *reading* the book, so I decided to go through with it. However, a little insight into WHY I even considered putting it on hold (and *seriously* entertained leaving the profession I love after 25 years) might shed some light on just how "easy" teaching is these days…

8a.m., Monday Morning, (A Nice but Anonymous for legal reasons) Hospital, Pennsylvania:

"I need to ask you a few questions, and your honesty will go a long way in helping us to determine what's going on with you." So sayeth the cardiologist that was trying to get to the bottom of my recent health "issues."

Yeah…like I had a chance of lying about *anything* with my wife— Dawn Stepnowski: DNP, APN-C, CBN—sitting next to me. In fact, it probably would have been easier if the doctors that were going to meet with me over the next few weeks just asked *her* the questions, because whatever *I* said was going to be (much to my chagrin) reanswered, corrected, and elaborated upon by Dr. Wife.

A little background may be in order. After being a smooth, compliant, healthy muscle for 45 years, my heart decided to (for no apparent reason, for extended moments at a time) start running like a NASCAR driver after a dozen espressos.

Nonetheless, here is a quick-fast-and-in-a-hurry synopsis of the Q&A I was subjected to, multiple times, over the course of a month or so:

Height and weight screening: 6'3" 265lbs.

Bodyfat percentage: 20% (Really? Well *that's* depressing…)

"Previous family history of cardiac issues/high blood pressure?" No.

"Do you smoke?" Never.

"Drugs?" Never.

"Never?" Unless you count Excedrin 3-4 times a year, *never.*

"Alcohol?" At most, a few glasses of wine or a few beers every few month.

"Caffeine intake?" 2-4 cups of black coffee a day.

"A Day?" Doc…I'm a teacher. By mid-November my *blood type* is coffee bean.

"Diet?" Hardly perfect, but very little sugar, limited white flour, a lot of water and protein…"

"Medical check-ups?" Regularly.

"How often do you exercise?" 4-5 days a week, religiously, for over 25 years.

"What kind?" Everything from powerlifting to Bikram yoga; lately, a lot of Crossfit.

and finally... *(Imagine dramatic, NLF-films documentary voice, with echo:)* **"What's your stress level like?" like—like—like—like?"** Well Doc, I teach High School English, and I'm the Dean of discipline for the freshmen, so I'd say my stress level is, I don't know, weapons grade nuclear?

OK, so we know you need to lower your caffeine intake and your stress level.

I'll repeat that, just so the teachers of the world can have a few moments to stop laughing hysterically: *You need to lower your caffeine intake and your stress level.*

Yeah, doc, I'll get right on that.

In the meantime, I'll endure what one physician described as "PTSD-type symptoms."

While I appreciate what the doc was trying to say, I know quite a few people that are, or were, active military, having served in war zones, and I won't claim to have experienced anything *remotely near* what they have, so post-traumatic stress disorder might be pushing it a bit.

HOWEVER...

Any teacher still active in the "trenches" will tell you—from elementary to post-secondary, from Honors to Special Ed., gym teacher to Quantum Physics professor—we deal with more confrontation and open hostility on a *daily* basis than most people do in a **lifetime.**

Don't believe me?

How many times have you been cursed out, loudly, in public? How many times have you had your life (or the lives of your family) threatened? How many times have you had to physically restrain someone? How many times have you had to wash someone else's blood out of your clothes? How many times have you had someone threaten to get you fired [for doing nothing but what your contract *requires*?] How many times have you had one of your employees tell you that he doesn't need to listen to you (and then been supported for saying it?) How many times have you spent your own money on materials for your job and then been chastised for "not having enough?" How many times have you been publicly accused of racism? How many times has your pay, or your benefits, been calculated incorrectly (and would have stayed that way had *you* not caught it and done the legwork to get it fixed?) How many times has someone confessed to you that they: were pregnant, were gay, had committed a crime, were going to kill themselves, were going to hurt someone else, etc. "but please don't tell anyone?"

Many of you would say: "Uh…never."

Most teachers would say "You mean *this* week?"

I could go on and on but I'll end with this: How many times have you been told that you are suffering, as a DIRECT RESULT of your job, from *Stress-Induced Susceptibility to Sudden Cardiac Death?*

I can answer that one.

Once.

But once is enough, don't you think?

I sure did. As a matter of fact, I thought to myself: "Self, you need to seriously consider getting out of this profession. It's killing you, quite literally; and if you do choose to stay, you REALLY need to consider scrapping this book and writing children's books or some stuff that will generate warm fuzzy feelings and a heart rate that doesn't sound like Meshuggah's rhythm section."

Then I thought, "Hey, there are probably a million other factors involved in this cardiac conspiracy" (teachers tend to be great at outsmarting ourselves) "I mean, after all, nobody else I work with is dealing with issues like this, are they?"

Are they?

They are.

Got FOUR names for you: (all changed to protect the innocent, of course)

Sarah Solubility, Kevin Yourisdaughter, Luis Amberwavesofgrain, and Thomas Honeycomb. All *very* young (heck of a lot younger than me, anyway,) all *very* healthy, all with *no* family history of heart shenanigans, and yet what do all of these people have in common?

Every one of them has, *in the past twenty-four months,* **had to wear a heart monitor.**

Different genders, races, ages, family status, job positions and personalities, and yet we all had stress-related symptoms stemming from the only thing we have in common—working in education.

I'm no detective, but I think we have found our culprit:

Mr. Step… in the classroom… with the gradebook! (Apologies to those of you too young to get the CLUE reference.)

Allusions to 1950s Hasbro board games aside, I had to throw out the "I'm suffering in isolation" theory and try to talk myself out of this another way. "Listen," I said to myself, "this is probably just a 'getting older' thing, or something I never noticed before; this is, in no way, a manifestation of my job, for crying out loud."

Wrong again, genius.

You see, my big ol' Flavor Flav heart monitor revealed some interesting stuff. Seems that my system went more haywire walking the halls at work than it did even during the most insane, hate-my-parents-for-giving-birth-to-me Crossfit workouts.

"Darn it," I said, to nobody in particular, "if stress is doing this to me, and this teaching thing gets more stressful every year, should I stop?"

Nah. I already told you in chapter one that I would die for one of your kids, so *(insert tearful, dramatic, Oscar-worthy voice with single tear trickling down the cheek of my good side,)* I'm certainly willing to check out on behalf of all of them.

Academy award winning monologues aside, know what else? Those four intrepid adventurers I mentioned earlier? Sarah, Kevin, Luis, and Thomas? They all would, too.

For real.

Know what else? I'll bet dollars to doughnuts that if you know a few people "in education," that at least one of them has some sort of stress-related physical manifestation that's hurting them.

Know what else? THEY keep going, too, because that's what we do.

Say it with me: Teaching sucks, but we love it.

PART XIII
MAGIC FLIGHT

Sometimes the hero returns home with the blessings of all and supported by the gods and his supernatural patrons; the final stage of his journey is an easy, " hail-the-conquering-hero" love-fest.

Sometimes…not so much.

In his *The Hero with a Thousand Faces*, Joseph Campbell points out that "If the hero's wish to return to the world has been resented by gods or demons, then the last stage of the mythological round becomes a lively, almost comical pursuit. This flight may be complicated by marvels of magical obstruction and evasion." (170)

Hmmm….Resented by demons? An almost comical pursuit, complicated by obstruction? I've never encountered anyth—

Wait a minute! I think I might have *just* the story for this chapter! Let me check my notes…I know it's here somewhere…Ah HA! Yes, this is *perfect*.

Might get me in trouble, though.

Ah the heck with it, this is too good not to share.

Soundtrack for the chapter—*The Hand that Feeds* —Nine Inch Nails

A Low Blow at the Dog and Pony Show.

Shortly after the tragedy that unfolded in Connecticut, a very high ranking administrator, who shall be hereafter known as Ms. Terious, showed up **in person** at our school, ready to overreact and posture (as did so many administrators across America.) God forbid they had been proactive and invisible, in keeping with the manner of people who are *truly* concerned about the safety of those in their charge.*

*Before you ask, yes I *do* know. I, myself, had some formal bodyguard training, and I am friends with men and women ranging from a S.W.A.T .captain to professional security experts. Their input is always practical, informative and extremely scary. Thanks to them, I can't enjoy my dinner at Chili's without assessing the possible exit strategies should someone open fire during my fajitas.

But I digress. Ms. Terious showed up ready to save the world (a day late and a dollar short,) armed with nothing but some unrealistic goals and a fiery desire to capitalize on the fear that an incident like the one at Sandy Hook Elementary inevitably generates. I'm not sure which of her escapades I enjoyed more, but here are a few of them, for your amusement.

Apparently, a student let her in the building on the day of her publicity tour. She asked him if she knew who she was. He said "no." So she promptly chastised him (publicly) for letting a stranger into the building (never mind that the "stranger" had three men in suits with her, all carrying clipboards and looking decidedly "non-psychotic shooter-type.) The poor kid was probably thinking *"I promise you, b----, that I will NEVER open the door for you again, and I hope you're out there in a rainstorm in your expensive shoes."* In the meantime, our heroine moved on, with intense purpose, never stopping to wonder WHY a student **didn't know** who she was;

maybe because he never saw her before?

Can't be bothered with *that* sort of minutiae can we? No sir, not when we can be busy doing things like trying to embarrass the auto shop teacher, by asking him, loudly and publicly, "why the [auto shop] doors [were] wide open," exposing the children to potential terrors. Fortunately, some of the more advanced students were there to inform her that they would die of carbon monoxide poisoning if the doors were shut, as it was, after all, *an auto shop*. The wood shop teacher was similarly interrogated for not coming to the door on time to address her highness; apparently, leaving a warehouse-sized room filled with kids of questionable maturity alone with a variety of power tools and *actively spinning saw blades* pales in comparison to getting to the door when the Big Cheese comes to visit.

I wish I could tell you that I managed to avoid direct encounter with this dog and pony show, and I wish I could tell you that when I did encounter it, I kept my mouth shut. But that just wouldn't be my luck, now would it?

But first, *an informative FLASHBACK:*

Within days of the unspeakable acts in Connecticut, the educational staff received a stunningly long Email detailing all of the new changes in our "security plan" that would be implemented immediately. It struck me odd that the first few PAGES seemed dedicated to getting teachers to swipe in with their new swipe cards every time they entered or exited the building (and signing in and out as well, in the interest of redundancy) and that any unauthorized swiping, signing or waxing on or off would result in possible termination.

I could go on and on, and I DID consider just reprinting some of the new policies for your amusement (my lawyers politely put *that* idea to rest) but let me get right to the point. Do some research on school shootings in the United States and, in addition to having your faith in humanity tested, you'll notice one striking similarity...

THE <u>TEACHERS</u> DIDN'T KILL ANYONE.

In fact, four young teachers *gave their lives* PROTECTING their students at Sandy Hook Elementary School. So why the sudden "Big Brother-ing" of the educational staff? I can only speak for myself, but to me it felt like a scholastic version of the Patriotic Act—taking advantage of people's recent and raw insecurities to further an agenda bent on unnecessary supervision of the innocent. In any event, I was (and remain) a big fan of Dora the Explorer—"Swiper no swiping!!"—so it was awfully hard for me to comply with such Orwellian ostentatiousness, despite the fact that my rakish smile came across *sooooo* photogenic on my swipe card.

And now we return to our regularly scheduled program

Ms. Terious was in the hallways, filled with zeal and attended by our school administrators, ALL of whom appeared absolutely thrilled to be engaged in such meaningful work the day before Christmas break when (as anybody in the profession knows) the kids are SO well behaved.

I, gentle reader, was on my way to use up my lunch period making three phone calls to parents that requested updates prior to the holiday, absolutely thrilled to be doing so on the day before Christmas break. Ms. Terious was right in front of me, as unavoidable as the troll beneath the bridge in so many fairy tales.

I should point out that *this* Billy Goats Gruff was, for the first time in over 20 years, actually sick (as in 102 degree fever, bronchial pneumonia-type sick) but I refused to call in sick out of sheer professional obligation to the school that was now *Big Brothering* me because of the actions of one psychotic twit. Baaaaaaad move.

Ah, but you know what they say; "no good deed goes unpunished."

I **should** have turned around and walked the other way. I **should** have declined comment, covered my mouth and said "I don't want to get you sick, too" and hurried on my way, and I most certainly **should not** have offered any commentary or criticism on Ms. Terious' oh-so-meaningful display of concern.

I know, I know…Mary Wilson, my dear old mom, always said "your mouth is going to make you famous or get you in a lot of trouble."

Me and my mouth tried to walk by Ms. Terious, but she accosted me, starting in the middle of a thought (as those enthralled with their inner dialogue are wont to do.)

"I'm going to get them down to 4 minutes."

"I don't know what that means." I replied, knowing what it meant but failing to listen to my own inner dialogue, which is usually full of crap.

"The students," she gestured to a High School hallway that looked like you think a High School hallway would look the day before Christmas break, *"I'm going to get them down to four minutes in the hallways. Yesterday, they were at 8 minutes, but today I've got them down to 6 minutes."*

It was at this moment that I was reminded of the words of Horace Walpole:

"The world is a comedy to those that think; a tragedy to those that feel."

Tragic in that *this* was the input from our Supreme Administrator in response to a tragedy of incomprehensible proportion; comedic that she thought she was making even a microscopic difference by showing up for a few days with a timer and rushing kids that didn't know who she was to classrooms they would have entered several seconds later anyway.

"Really? What's your **plan** for that?" I inquired, my sarcasm thinly veiled beneath a haze of fever-induced vapor.

She didn't seem to like that she had been greeted with inquiry instead of acquiescence, but recovered quickly: *"Well, a wise man once said that 'the first step is **believing** that it can be done!'"* (Cue dramatic sweeping hand gesture.)

"Well,"

I couldn't resist,

"A wiser man than I once said that a 'goal without a plan is just a wish,' but I **wish** you luck, and a happy holiday" and off I went to make phone calls while I drank my lunch.

Famous—0 Trouble—1 Sorry, Mom.

"Mister Stepnowski," she called, with all the grace of a cobra asking a mongoose how that broken leg was coming along, *"if you were in charge,* (a subtle reminder that I was NOT,) *what would be YOUR plan* (she said the word *plan* like she has swallowed a bad oyster) *to get kids out of the hallways?"*

The French have a lovely word for that moment—too late, AFTER a verbal exchange—when you think of the perfect thing to say; they call it *L'esprit d'escalier* and I, like you, have experienced this more times than I care to admit.

This wasn't one of those times. For once, I knew exactly what I wanted to say at the exact moment I wanted to say it:

"I'd start by creating a classroom environment that kids **wanted** to get to so they **wouldn't** linger in the halls. (Cue mockingly dramatic hand gesture) Been there, DONE that and, if you'll excuse me, I'm late getting **TO** it."

And with that I was off, literally burning up with fever, having metaphorically shredded my ticket to the dog and pony show. I suspect that many of my fellow educators have put their job security a little too close to the fire by, in a moment of consummate frustration, *telling it like it is* instead of just playing ball and singing along with the circus music.

Later that evening, as I stretched out on the floor (always makes me feel better, don't ask me why) it occurred to me that I had, indeed, "crossed the return threshold." I was weapons-grade pissed off, I wasn't afraid of being fired for speaking my mind because I KNEW that what I was doing was *right* and, infinitely more importantly, I finally felt confident that if not one person read this book, I would still feel better for having published it. (And hasn't that more or less become the **theme** of this little book here?)

Duly inspired, I eventually stopped burning up like the Human Torch, coughing up blood like Bill Compton and congratulating myself for fitting a *Marvel Comics* AND *True Blood* allusion into one sentence—and I sent Emails to my publisher, my editor, and my graphics guy: "Book three will be a reality within a few weeks, folks, let's get moving."

I'm coming home.

PART XIV
RESCUE FROM WITHOUT

Sometimes, the hero is so entrenched in his supernatural journey, he needs a powerful guide to "bring him back to reality" (especially if he's been wounded or weakened during his journey.)

Whenever I'm lost, overwhelmed, embittered, or just feel like I don't know what to do next as a teacher, I often find direction, salvation and inspiration in the words of others, whether they come from the printed page, or in conversations with my fellow citizens.

Soundtrack for this chapter: *Don't get Me Started* —Rodney Crowell

Dining, Doctors, Doughnuts, and Digested Lambs.

I think we all need to listen to the "voices of reason" around us from time to time. I speak with some degree of authority when I say that teachers in particular are so used to doing the talking that we often forget what Bruce Lee taught us, that: "A wise man can learn more from a foolish question than a fool can learn from a wise answer." This is not to say that we need to seek out "foolish" people, not at all; I am simply telling you that—sometimes—the things we need to hear often come from the most unexpected places, IF we are but willing to slow down, suppress our egos, and *listen*.

Let me tell you about some "voices of reason" (from what you may consider unlikely sources) that came to my aid when I was frustrated and running on empty, my "rescue from without" if you will: The restaurant business, the medical industry, the place where I buy my morning coffee, and books. You *know* I love me some alliteration, so…

Dining, **D**octors, and **D**oughnuts, and **D**igested Lambs.

When people ask me about books I've read that were pleasant surprises, one of the first ones that *always* comes to mind is Anthony

Bourdain's *Kitchen Confidential;* a full-frontal, non-apologetic, look behind the curtain of the restaurant business. Bourdain's maiden voyage into writing is, to put it mildly, terrifyingly [but intoxicatingly] informative; in fact, one of the greatest compliments I ever received was when someone said that my first book, "...*with the laughs, profanity, and brutal honesty, should have been called Classroom Confidential!*" When my friend Marc Granieri heard about our mutual appreciation of the book, he lent me two of Bourdain's other books—*The Nasty Bits* and *Medium Raw,* along with another brutally insightful book, *Waiter Rant* by Steve Dublanica. (A few times, in the middle of *Waiter Rant,* I thought "me and this guy must've compared notes in some former life.") The raw reality of these books reminded me that teaching is NOT the only profession where:

- the hardest workers are often paid the least amount of money, and
- those blue collar workers are VERY often abused by a population that takes their own frustrations [about their lives] out on them.
- The people "in charge" forgot everything they knew to be true "in the trenches" the minute they got a "supervisory" position.
- The behind-the-scenes reality that truly "gets the job done" is not something the public wants to know about.
- The pressures of dealing with the public face-to-face on a continual basis lead to a variety of physical/psychological issues and self-destructive behaviors.

When you live in a vacuum—and if you teach and have *any* kind of life outside the classroom, you do—it's always nice to know that you aren't alone.

Thank you, Tony; thank you Steve.

Of course, people in the food services business work in equal measure with animate and inanimate objects and, (to be honest,) people *could* stop going out to eat.

People *can't* stop getting sick.

Which brings us to the medical profession.

Perhaps more than any other, the workers in the medical profession understand the plight of those" in education" (which may explain why teachers and nurses often cohabitate in the wild.)

We both deal with a population that we *must, by law,* care for, regardless of how thankless, rude, and ungrateful they are. Key word: CARE. We can't "alter" your food, "forget" to put an item in your bag, rob you blind with "helpful" advice or any of the other dirtier tricks of the retail, deal-with-the-public trade.

If educational personnel don't give our very best, a kid can be irreversibly damaged at a key developmental point in their intellectual/psychological/social development. If medical personnel slack in the caring department, someone *dies.*

So we **care**, which makes it even more obnoxious when we have to deal with "concerned" family members who compromise the care of their loved ones by harassing us and telling us how to do the job that NO ONE in their circle of influence is even *remotely* qualified to do.*

*NOTE: My advisors told me to "tone this down" a bit and this is the <u>only</u> time I didn't listen to their advice. Many of my friends are teachers, and I *live* with a nurse and a doctor so I'm privy to FAR too many stories of ignorant, uneducated people (whose lack of social skills is the only thing that outweighs their lack of education) profanely, obnoxiously telling medical and educational staff how to "do their job."

Screw you. Do *your* job.

Sorry. Fangs retracted, back to business.

While I can't say it makes me feel any better to know that nurses are taking it on the chin as badly, or worse, than we are—it nonetheless confirms my fear that the people dealing with "human product" are, with frightening increase, being told what to do by bean counters that simply do not give a rat's ass about our students, patients, or coffee customers.

"Yeah, Step! You tell 'em!" you shout (in my dreams) "Somebody needs to…wait…did you say *coffee customers?*"

I did, and with that I introduce another source of sympathy to our cause; specifically, the staff of the Dunkin' Donuts where I purchase, with frightening regularity, my morning large black coffee and, on Fridays, two sour cream doughnuts.

Don't judge me, you bastards, I am weak once a week.

Sometimes twice.

Long story short, the gang that, for longer than I can remember, served me up my caffeine and carbohydrates, did so happily and with the kind of easy precision that comes from working together for years and working in a pleasant, light-hearted environment.

Shiva, Vishnu and Brahma (2/3 of which are their *real names* so stick it if you think I'm stereotyping) always gave me the smiles and small talk I needed at 6 am on my way to a day of teaching teenagers, and they did as such for everyone else, which is probably why—with 2 other Dunkin' Donuts franchises within mere minutes of this one—there was always a line to get served at "my" DD.

Then, about 6 months ago, the smiles gave way to palpable tension and the small talk turned into sales pitches and "upgrade offers." The occasional "here's a free doughnut for your little girl in addition to your dozen" and "see you tomorrow, buddy" was replaced by an automatic change spitting register and a layer of cream cheese on the bagels so thin that you could read through it.

Know what *else* showed up around that time? A new face; a younger (than the staff) but clearly "superior" drone from the DD

Death Star headquarters here to ensure that extra napkins were accounted for and EVERY coffee came with a *"do you want a doughnut with that?"* or *"we have gift cards available."*

Ah…where have we seen *this* before? The old *"it-ain't-broke-so-let's-fix-the-hell-out-of-it"* business model. Do I need to tell you what's happening to the lines at my beloved coffee stop? I still go there, and still share winks and conspiratorial smiles with Vish, Shiv and B. when they serve me (especially when the sour cream stormtrooper ain't around.) Nonetheless, it is a sober reminder that we're all fighting the same good fight.

This brings us, with delicious finality, to what has ALWAYS been my rescue when I needed it—books; specifically, some of the books that slapped me back into sense whilst writing this particular poor excuse for literature.

Seriously Step? Dedicating several pages of a chapter to book recommendations? For **this** *I paid my hard earned money?*

Well, I'd like to think that you plopped down your pesos for this proliferation of platitudes because you're a nice, literate person that shares my interests and loves Pina Coladas and getting caught in the rain. Besides, haven't you been paying attention?? Reading is the single most important factor in your intellectual and/or professional development, so listen up.

And, if it helps, just think of me as all your "bad librarian" fantasies come to life.

You, too, ladies.

Fellow educators—I am acutely aware of an increasing trend that, as appalling as it is, is even more damaging to the profession we love so dearly. Far too many teachers, themselves, don't read independently; and if they *are* reading, none of their choices are professional in nature.

According to Jim Trelease, in his book *The Read Aloud Handbook:* "teachers… read few or no professional journals that included research. More than half...read only one or two professional books in the previous year, and an additional 20 percent said that *they had read nothing* in the last six months or one year." (100-101)

Furthermore, The Pew Research Center unveiled, in a 2012 study, that the ***median number*** of books consumed, in a ***year***, by Americans was ***six.***

Come *on*, people; we're better than that.

Books replenish my strength and combat the kryptonite of exhaustion. Many of the professional books I read infuriate, inspire, or (at the very least) interest me enough to shake me out of the doldrums.

Consequently, I felt compelled to share some of the works that kept me going during the writing of this here literary masterpiece. Kidding aside, no matter how much my big mouth talks, I can pretty much guarantee that someone has said it better—or at least more succinctly/professionally—before me. That having been said, here are some titles and authors that "rescued *me* from without" and that might do the same for you. If you're ready to flip ahead because "you're not 'into' reading," let me remind you of the words of Harlan Ellison, who observed, correctly, that *"We're dealing with a more and more illiterate and amnesiac constituency. It's impossible to get a readership that will follow you, because all they know is what they knew yesterday."*

Once *again*, come on, people; we're better than that. So here are some eye-opening texts you might find interesting and rejuvenating:

<u>Want to know why our educational system is more broken than Batman after Bane got done with him?</u>

- ***The Death and Life of the Great American School System: How Testing and Choice Are Undermining Education*** and ***The Language Police: How Pressure Groups Restrict What Students Learn***—Diane Ravitch

- *Below C Level: How American Education Encourages Mediocrity and What We Can Do About It* —John Merrow
- *Many Children Left Behind:* —Deborah Meier and George Wood
- *Weapons of Mass Instruction* and *Dumbing Us Down: The Hidden Curriculum of Compulsory Schooling* —John Taylor Gatto
- *Pedagogy of the Oppressed* —Paulo Freire
- *The Homework Myth: Why Our Kids Get Too Much of a Bad Thing* and *The Case Against Standardized Testing* —Alfie Kohn
- *The Future of our Schools* —Lois Weiner

Want some diverse insight into our student population (that you may not want to hear?)

- *Children of the Core* —Kris Nielsen
- *Losing Heart: The Moral and Spiritual Miseducation of America's Children* —H. Svi Shapiro
- *Nurture Shock; New Thinking About Children* —Po Bronson and Ashley Merryman
- *Doing School: How We Are Creating a Generation of Stressed-Out, Materialistic, and Mis-educated Students* —Denise Clark Pope
- *The Dumbest Generation: How the Digital Age Stupefies Young Americans and Jeopardizes Our Future.* —Mark Bauerlein
- *Class and Schools* —Richard Rothstein

How about some advice on getting (your real kids or your students) to read?

- *Readicide* and *Deeper Reading* —Kelly Gallagher
- *Book Love* —Penny Kittle
- *When Kids Can't Read* —Kylene Beers
- *I Read it, but I Don't Get It* —Chris Tovani

Looking for a book that transcends genres, classrooms, and cultures—I have used this book countless times to teach (and remind myself to practice) tolerance and self-awareness.

- **Powerful Peace: A Navy SEAL's Lessons on Peace from a Lifetime at War** —J. Robert DuBois

It should go without saying that I could go on and on and on but, instead, I'll simply recommend that you check out Sir Ken Robinson's video **"Changing Educational Paradigms"** and Taylor Mail's video **"What Teachers Make"** on TED.com to get your grey matter fired up to get back to work; in the interim, if you have anything you think I should read, reach out on Facebook or Twitter and let me know. Seriously, let me know, 'cause by mid-year, I'll probably need some "rescue" again.

Oh, almost forgot—you probably want to know why this section is called "Digested Lambs" huh? Good for you for being so inquisitive! You must read a lot. The title comes from Charles de Gaulle who, when asked about his literary influences, responded: *"Don't ask me who's influenced me. A lion is made up of the lambs he's digested, and I've been reading all my life."*

I hope you lions out there have lots of lambs in your future, and I'm very honored to know that this book is in your belly.

PART XV
CROSSING
THE RETURN THRESHOLD

Retaining the wisdom he has obtained on his quest, the hero must integrate that wisdom into his "normal," non-heroic life, and possibly *share* that knowledge with the rest of the world.

How to take the lessons I've learned on my "journey" and bring them home? Fortunately for me, my son Mason and I had some yard work to do, and—to quote Ben Stein—sometimes you just have to "jump into the middle of things, get your hands dirty, fall flat on your face, and **then** reach for the stars."

Turns out all it took was some stinky mulch and a great kid to bring it all together.

Soundtrack for the chapter—*I Can See Clearly Now* —Johnny Nash

GETTING DIRTY
(lessons in teaching learned among the stinky stuff).

You can learn a lot about teaching by doing yard work.

Allow me to explain. Spring has recently sprung, and on my way home from work today, I decided, in light of my wife's exceptional efforts to make everyone in the house comfortable of late [despite a crippling work schedule of her own,] to surprise her by getting the property around our house all beautiful and stuff. I'd been sneaking in some weeding and thatching and the like over the last week so it was just about time for my favorite yard work—mulching.

Teaching Lesson #1—if you have a good (read: supportive) boss, occasionally reward them with effort above and beyond, even if it is at the expense of your time and money.

Allow me to explain, lest you think I'm somehow wrong in the head for *enjoying* having a small mountain of stinky root mulch dropped smack dab in the middle of my driveway (and the subsequent back breaking work required to shovel, transport, and spread it properly over a large property, not to mention the cleanup.)

OK, when you put it that way, maybe I *am* wrong in the head, but let me explain nonetheless. And before you start—no, I do not assume everyone has a lawn, or even a yard, or even a live plant, but I'm metaphoring here, so quiet down and embrace the lesson, will ya?

3:15 pm, and a very large man is dropping off the 12 yards of black mulch I ordered into my driveway with a very large truck, earning him a very large tip for getting this puppy here with enough daylight that my son Mason (15) and I can get this job done by nightfall. When I remarked as such, the guy dropping off this brontosaurus-turd-sized pile chuckled, noting that *"that was a LOT of mulch"* and *"that we probably wouldn't get [it] done by this [evening.]"* I smiled back and asked him when he was done work. When he told me 8pm, I asked him to cruise by on his way home and see if there was any mulch in this driveway. He laughed, shook my hand, saluted Mason, and wished us Godspeed.

As soon as he pulled away, Mason looked at me, glanced around at the two wheelbarrows, rakes, shovels, etc. and smirked. *"I was thinking **way** before 8:00"* was all he said. I returned the smile, and one fist bump later, the iPod was blaring, and the furious sound of shoveling echoed around the block. It was 3:30 pm.

Teaching Lesson #2—There is a certain confidence that comes from having your materials organized, and having honed your craft through years of trial and error.

Teaching Lesson #3—Putting in a lot, and I mean a LOT of time and effort with a student will—almost always—pay huge dividends. <u>I am a slave driver when it comes to my kids, always have been</u>, <u>but I also took the time—EVERY SINGLE TIME—to explain the *WHEREs* and *WHYs* of everything we *ever* did</u>. <u>It was unbelievably time con-suming</u>, <u>excruciatingly repetitive</u> (and <u>mind-numbingly frustrating,</u> when they had to be reminded of something you JUST taught them yesterday…)

But it works. As a result, my 15 yr.-old son (and his 14 yr.-old brother, for the record,) EACH work like *two* full grown men and, more importantly, we have an unspoken, symbiotic communication that ONLY comes from putting in time with a person, and is *necessary* when you're trying to get a ton of work done in record time (and isn't every teacher?)

5:30 pm, on schedule but starting to get tired. Mason is tired, too, but neither one of us will admit it. We are working for something bigger than ourselves, we are thoroughly enjoying our time together in the sun, and, truth be told, we are determined to prove the mulch delivery guy wrong. No words needed be spoken, much shoveling, wheel barrowing and raking to be done...

Teaching Lesson #4—Motivation comes in many forms: embrace that fact when working with a roomful of students; again, it's a LOT of work, but it beats having your charges "tune out" all year long. Know what will keep your students motivated and you'll all have a more satisfying time.

Approximately 6:00. The last thing I want to do on my end is slow down and mulch around little flowers and newly sprouting vegetation by hand, it would be so much easier to just toss it around; and after all, nobody looks that close, so who would know?

Answer: I would; and so it's onto my knees, carefully fluffing mulch in between leaves and delicate shoots and stems. At least the music is going strong...

Meanwhile, Mas is getting held up on his side having to rake old, moldy leaves stuck in tight spots out of the way and drag them to the street. It would be so much easier to just dump mulch over the leaves, and who would know?

Answer: He would, and I cursed him with the burden of personal accountability, so it's rake and haul time before he can get back to the job at hand. At least the sun is still out, and Mom isn't home yet…

Teaching Lesson #5—The little things matter.

- **Take those 5 minutes to Email a parent to let them know their kid did something *right* (when all you want to do is watch 5 minutes of television.)**
- **I know you wanted to try to get 8 *actual* hours of sleep to-night (believe me I know) but *you know* you should get those papers corrected so you can go over them tomorrow while they're fresh in the student's heads.**
- **No, Ms. Joyce, (or whoever makes *your* copies for you when you're desperate and need them yesterday) thank YOU, and yes, I know how you like your coffee. No, ma'am, it's no trouble at all—*thank you.***

After all, who would know?
Answer: Everyone, and that's what elevates the teachers who care—there's nothing "hidden under their mulch"

And speaking of mulch… it's almost 7:00, sun's going down slowly and Mom will be pulling in from work any second and we've still got about a yard left in the driveway ($?#&*@! weeds) but I can see the fire in Mason's eyes and I know just how to make sure it doesn't extinguish. "Hey Mayo, we have to return this leaf blower to the Hossler's when we're done, and Rita's Water Ice is on the way to their house…"

I suddenly have my son's undivided attention

"so you knock out that last patch, I'll start cleaning up and putting everything back in the shed…"

Mason is gone, in a flash, shoveling like a man possessed.

Teaching Lesson #6—TANGIBLY reward exceptional effort. (Even if it means a *Swedish Fish* flavored water ice Gelati *before* dinner.) Rules must, occasionally, be broken in the face of great performance.

7:15 Mom pulls up. She is pleased. I *know* she wants to ask if we weeded thoroughly before we put down the mulch, I *know* she wants to walk around the property to see if we did it "right," (grrrrrrrrr) and I *know* she is concerned about the black stain in our driveway finding its way into our house... But she knows, from past experience, what that will do and, as I said, she is pleased, so she smiles, says it looks beautiful, and tells us she will make us a delicious dinner.

Teaching Lesson #7—Sometimes you gotta resist the temptation to micromanage. YOU know that you want your students to improve continuously, and they know it, too, but sometimes (and you'll know when) you just have to smile (sometimes through gritted teeth) and say "good job."

7:30—TWELVE YARDS of mulch distributed over a very nice looking (if I do say so myself) property IN 4 HOURS *just as we knew it would be.* Mason and I finish up the little details—**always finish as strong as you started**—and it's off to return the super-powered leaf blower I borrow, faithfully, every Spring, from my friends the Hosslers, who cheerfully hand it over, primed, fully gassed and ready to rock.

Teaching Lesson #8—You can't do it alone. I tried. You break yourself down and hurt everyone's feeling in the process. Then you're worthless and everybody is pissed at you. People *want* to help, and they wouldn't be your friends if they weren't pretty good people, so let 'em help—the quality of your work can only benefit. Of course, *quid pro quo,* help them when they need it.

Back home, with just enough light left to appreciate a job well done. Mom sees the water ice and says nothing (she, too, is a fierce leader that understands the necessity of the occasional broken "rule;" *AND she knows we'll still eat plenty of dinner.*) The siblings ask, before they have time to think, where *their* treats are....

Judging from the looks on their faces, they know the answer. I don't even have to say it, but I do anyway: *"**Yours** were under **YOUR** shovels outside, but since **you** never picked them up..."*

Nobody argues.

They know better, and they know they'll be on the other end sooner than later.

Teaching Lesson #8—There are no weak soldiers under a strong general. Kids can handle a LOT more than the people who would feign to "save" them think they can. Your students will appreciate the faith you have in their ability to withstand criticism, it will make them stronger (or, in some cases, break them, and that isn't always a bad thing.)

After dinner, Mas and I head upstairs to clean up our nasty-looking/smelling selves, as we head into our respective bathrooms, Mas raises his hand for a high-five, which I gladly reciprocate.

"Can't get it done by tonight? What's he thinking?"

"He clearly doesn't know how hard we work, Mayo; remember, most kids your age don't have your work ethic."

"Most kids didn't have you for a dad." And off he went.

Teaching Lesson #9—It's worth it. It's worth it. It is *so* worth it.

PART XVI
MASTER OF TWO WORLDS

In this step, our intrepid hero achieves balance between the material and the spiritual. The hero becomes comfortable and competent with both his inner world and the machinations of the outer world.

My father is extremely wise, and pretty successful, for a guy that didn't have any post-secondary education (which, in itself, speaks to what I've been saying about our educational system.)

Most of my complaints growing up were met with a simple response: "Any lazy idiot can complain. Do not complain about a problem unless you *have a solution* and are **willing to work** *to make it happen.*"

So, when the teacher that complained long and loud about administrators was offered the chance to (sort of) join the ranks? Put up or shut up, buddy—time to become the master of two worlds.

Soundtrack for this chapter: *Best of Both Worlds* —Van Halen

Lean, Mean, and…You want ME to be a Dean?!

So there I was (always wanted to start a chapter like that) and it was a dark and stormy night (not really, but I figured why not get TWO cliché' beginnings in with one shot.)

Mid-July, 2011. So there I was, on my way to pick up a few Power Bars for tomorrow's 'breakfast' as I was running in my first ever Spartan Race (one of those crazy obstacle races that's part marathon, part survival test, 100% fun and 0% sane.) I was excited and nervous and jacked up on adrenaline. So when my cell phone rang and my then principal, Dennis Venison, asked if I was in the area and "could I come in today for a private conversation?" my Spider senses, to put it mildly, started tingling.

It didn't make it any better when the only secretary working (mid-July, remember) just pointed to the office without looking up when I walked in the door, adding to the cryptic nature of the whole affair. When I walked in Mr. Venison, the 9th grade Vice Principal, Tracey Twister, and the director of personnel were smiling.

Hmmmm… take one teacher that is routinely "pushing the envelope," who has been running and eating a strict diet (both of which make me very, very unpleasant) for the first 4 weeks of his "vacation," and call him to an impromptu, and seemingly clandestine, meeting in July (that has all the earmarks of a professional termination) and you will get yourself a few seriously tense seconds prior to said meeting.

"Hey, thanks for coming" smiled Dennis, "glad we caught you in the neighborhood" as he stood to shake my hand.

"Yeah, Step" chimed in Tracey, "you lookin' tan and happy. I bet the kids are enjoying having you around for the Summer?"

OK...my homicidal impulses having been instantly dissuaded, now I was 100% free to be nothing but curious, so I got right down to it (semi-jokingly) as I sat down: "So what's going on, guys? Is this where I get fired for the stuff in book 2?"

They laughed, "no, I actually *liked* book 2," lied Dennis, "No, we're creating a new position for each grade level, and we want to ask you if you would consider being the Dean of students for the 9th grade."

Ms. Twister continued, "Yours was one of the first names that came up, Step; we think you would be great at this."

Hmmmm… take one teacher who was ready for a confrontation, who has *published books discussing his confrontations with administrators*, call him to a spontaneous meeting and offer him a semi-administrative position, and you will get yourself a fairly lengthy awkward silence during said meeting.

Silence broken, I got right down to business:

"Two things: One, do we have a specific job description for this Dean position? Two, assuming I take the position, you don't think that giving me a *title* is going to suddenly make me 'play nice' (I even made those annoying "air quotation marks" with my fingers) all the time, right?"

NOTE: Yes, in hindsight, I realize that I was being an unnecessarily distrustful ass.

Thankfully, my immaturity did not, to their enormous credit, dissuade any of the powers-that-be from extending the offer again and, after some shockingly good-natured dialogue, I accepted. I was, along with my standard teaching duties, to serve as the Dean of the [approximately 350] incoming freshmen. This meant that I would, one period a day, assist the 9th grade vice principal—the aforementioned Ms. Twister—in dealing with the daily slew of incoming discipline referrals. Ostensibly, the Deans (one per grade level) were to deal with "lower level infractions:" cutting, excessive late to class, electronic device usage, mild insubordinations, etc. so as to free up the VPs to handle the more serious stuff in a timely manner. We would meet with students (and, if need be, teachers) and then have the authority to issue (or rescind) detentions and, on occasion, in-school suspensions. Out of school suspension-worthy offenses and "high flyers" with excessive write-ups were exclusively handled by the vice principals. I had just enough power to facilitate real change, but not so much authority that a change in salary or schedule would be necessary.

Sounds good on paper, but then so does your fantasy football team.

I spoke to a LOT of teachers, nation-wide, in my research for this book, and I know that there are, believe it or not, many schools where the administrators do, in fact, have a good deal of time to serve as educational leaders because they aren't besieged by a tsunami of discipline reports.

My school is not one of them.

Within two *weeks* we had over 50 referrals ranging from "refused to put the phone away in class" to "screamed (****) you, you (*******) ing piece of (****,) then *threw hot coffee on me* while I was holding my laptop."

And these were the *incoming 9th graders,* who generally spent the first week of school trying not to get lost or soil their underwear. The juniors and seniors were already in mid-season form, but I had a job to do, so, for now, it was focus on freshmen time.

Kind of like Blade, the half-vampire, half-human that can "walk in both worlds," I started to see things from two very different perspectives. I had always seen every scholastic event through the eyes of both teacher and parent, but those are, or should be, very similar viewpoints. Over the next few weeks, as I worked my way into the Dean position, I gained some invaluable insight into the administrative side of our profession, a good deal of which I felt compelled to pass on to my fellow teachers. With your permission, I will share some of the insight I gained walking in both worlds.

The first thing that I noticed was that the administrators were, in a manner of speaking, "closer to the sun." To explain, when my wife and I were on vacation, we were warned that near the equator, the sun's rays don't have to travel as far to reach more Northern latitudes, so they deliver more UV rays per exposure time; hence, more efficient and more painful sunburn. I got to see, first hand, how the principals and vice principals were "directly exposed," if you will, to the heat coming down from the Evil Empire that I've been demonizing throughout this book. We teachers feel the heat for certain in the classroom, with the incessant testing, the common core standards that we're *told* to teach, the constant cuts to our resources, etc.; however, I got to see, first hand, the amount of time the admins spend filling out stacks of [what I found to be] useless paperwork designed to keep the metaphorical wolves at bay.

Speaking of paperwork, I was unpleasantly surprised to see how many trees are killed every time a student diagnosed as special ed. gets disciplined for doing something wrong. Example: I met with a student (let's call him Apollo Greed) several times during October and November about a variety of infractions that started to get worse and worse. The last time I saw him he received an in-school suspension, which he cut and—on the same day as the cut suspension—cursed out a female teacher, after refusing (for the umpteenth time) to stop talking over the teachers and listening to his iPod in class, and telling her that, and I quote: *"you ain't (expletive) and neither is your class."*

Because Mr. Greed was labeled as having "special needs," the 11th grade vice principal and her secretary had to fill out a seven page document, get approval from on high, and waste approximately four hours doing so to simply hold a young "man" (with a history of this type of behavior) accountable for being rude, profane, insubordinate and a distraction to the learning of 20 other kids. All this, of course, takes up valuable time that could be spent attending to other disciplinary issues that were accumulating throughout the day.

MANY of the administrators I spoke to in researching this book were very up front about how disappointed they were when they found out how much of their day was spent dealing with disciplinary issues (when they thought it would involve helping teachers and empowering students.) In fact, one of my friends, a former English teacher, Thomas Honeycomb—yes, he of the heart condition in part 12 of this very book—aged *noticeably* in one year after his move from the classroom to the vice principal's office. (Sorry Tommy, but you know it's true.) And every time he comes into classrooms for teacher observations, I see in his eyes the longing to be back in front of a classroom and students and away from a desk and a phone that never stops ringing.

And speaking of a phone that never stops ringing, as I was putting the finishing touches on this literary disasterpiece, my friend and (now former) principal, Mr. Dennis Venison announced that he was following in the footsteps of so many principals I've worked with by "moving on to a different position/location for a variety of reasons."

NOTE: You know how when a celebrity's PR people <u>say</u> that the 'star' is "taking time off for unspecified illness" we all <u>hear</u> "drug and alcohol rehab?" Yeah...when administrators say they're "moving on" from somewhere "for a variety of reasons" they're usually doing it because they can't stand the hailstorm of feces raining down on them from the only people closer to the sun than *they* are.

PART XVI: MASTER OF TWO WORLDS | 241

Alas, another one bites the dust: Godspeed, young man, and keep an English position in your new home for when this book is published and I get sued for assault with a deadly metaphor.

"Whoa whoa WHOA!" I hear some of you shouting, "Is this chapter actually expressing

sympathy? For *administrators*?? From *Frank Stepnowski*?!?" Hey, anything can happen on the

journey to self-awareness, ladies and gentlemen.

Administrators, from what I can see, fall into one of two categories: The career office dwellers that will do anything (including blatantly screwing over their subordinates) to maintain their beloved titles, and the ones that live in a constant state of *why-the-hell-can't-I-just-run-my-school (where I know the people better than anyone) the-way-I-KNOW-it-should-be-run?*

If you know any principals, vice principals or Deans, ask 'em if they agree with my administrative dichotomy, ok? I'd ask myself but the suits tend to generally ~~fear~~ avoid my books.

Now where was I (before I gave you the SparkNotes version of *Why Administrators are People Too?*) Ah yes… walking in both worlds. My two years and counting of Deanly duty have armed me with more than enough material to write another hilarious expose'-type book like my first one. More importantly, it has forced me to look—like Joni Mitchell—"at love from both sides now." I took full advantage of my opportunity to talk, in private, with kids that were already 'in trouble' to find out WHY (there I go again, asking questions…) they "didn't care" or "hated school" or why they thought sitting in detention was *far* preferable to sitting in class. I have, in my teaching gig, spoken to *legions* of kids about whatever was weighing heavy on their minds, but this was different—these kids perceived that, by just being in front of me, they had nothing to lose, so their "edit button" (if they ever *had* one) was noticeably absent.

Full frontal honesty.

Perfect.

In some cases, my reputation preceded me and the kid(s) would know that I was willing to listen to them, provided they addressed me in a respectful manner. Many of these kids, however, didn't know me or of me yet, so they thought I was just another full of crap authority figure ready to pretend to listen before dropping a pink slip on them. I found it fascinating that when I told them "I'm writing another book and I'm really curious to hear what you have to say about (insert topic)" that they, almost always, toned it down, made eye contact, and spoke honestly, if not eloquently about what was pissing them off and why they got in trouble so much.

Interesting... most of our students can/will talk to us the way we *want* them to talk to us *when they think someone is actually listening to them*. Could there be so many people **not** listening that these kids are perpetually jaded going into any conversation with an adult regarding their education?

Uh, yeah.

So WHO's not listening? Oh I don't know...

maybe the politicians, parents, teachers, peers, administrators and educational reformers/investors that I've been talking about on this literary journey to enlightenment?

Listen folks, I'll say it again—we are all in this together, and educating kids starts and ends with *the kids*. So we've got to listen to what they say and, sometimes,

most times,

what they say without actually saying, know what I mean?

Listening to a veritable conga line of kids *every single day* that got in trouble simply because they didn't care what happened to them in school because they didn't care about what happened to them at home because they were being "raised" by people that went adrift through the same cycle of hopelessness, (and knowing that 3 other

Deans and 4 vice principals and a head principal were doing the same *EVERY SINGLE DAY,*) **will** provide some unique insight, I assure you.

More than anything, it confirmed my omnipresent assertion that a whole heapin' LOT of the people involved DIRECTLY in educating our youth *do* care about them and *do* want to do a good job, they just:

1. Don't know how, or
2. they've become so jaded (thanks to years of the same educational runaround) or
3. they've become so concerned with self-preservation (thanks to programs like *No Child Left Behind* and *Race to the Top*) or
4. they've become so distrustful of one another (thanks to our "us" vs. "them" mentality) that they won't *work* ***together*** to ensure the best outcome for the kids.

Our time together is running out, but let me share with you three short stories that I was made privy to (thanks to my Dean position,) that shed unpleasantly stark light on *exactly* why we—the teachers—need to keep fighting the good fight for our kids, because nobody else seems to be.

Sad but true story #1—Useless Jordache genes

I had a student named Jordache Blue who was (despite being a Senior) transferred into my 11th grade College Prep English class after the first marking period. This is fairly common practice for students that need certain classes to graduate. JB received an 88 from her English teacher for her first marking period efforts, so that grade transferred and, since my name was now on her report card it appeared, to the entire world, as though she earned that in *my* class. She didn't;

in fact, I can honestly say that I have lost any shred of respect for the teacher that had Jordache prior to me because,

and I say this without an *ounce* of exaggeration,

this young lady wouldn't have had a **prayer** *of passing my son's 8th grade English class,* let alone MY 11th grade College Prep English Class. In fact, I'm pretty sure they *put* her in my class to "stick it to me" (for trying to raise awareness about the "50 on the report card no matter what" policy.) You see, her three *guaranteed* 50s, plus her 88, would give her 238 points, which would then be rounded up to a 240, which is sufficient to pass based on my school district's standards.

Jordache received a 40, a 27, and a *15* for her stellar efforts in my class for three marking periods. I called home, complained to the counseling department, sent interoffice Emails, wrote letters, saved assignments, <u>and documented</u> *everything* (<u>names</u>, <u>times</u>, <u>etc.</u>)

Of course, we all know what happened. Three magical upgrades later and Jordache Blue was getting fitted for a cap and gown. That, ladies and gentlemen, is a (expletive) joke. Sadly, *pathetically*, not as big a joke as the response I overheard when I called (as the Dean) to inquire about Jordache's intellectual well-being.

First I called (as Frank Stepnowski, concerned English teacher) her guidance counselor Yoosluss B. Jonez, and asked him if there was any way we could get this girl some tutoring or something because she didn't really pass English at the...

I was interrupted by a curt, highly anxious explanation of how "grades were in, senior failures could not be accepted at this time, and graduation practice was being scheduled and ..."

HE was interrupted by 22 words and a loud noise "I am well aware of school policy, I've been here longer than you. I was asking you to care about the *kid".* CLICK.

QUESTION: Did you use your fingers to count the words? Ha! I'll bet you did. That's cool.

Not so cool was the fact that YBJ didn't even call me back to argue, defend himself, express outrage at my rude hanging up on him. Nothing. Nada. Nyet.

Sooooooo I called the office of Mr. Yoosluss B. Jonez, guidance counselor extraordinaire, a few days later to inquire about the graduation status of several students. Of course, (sneaky cheeky monkey that I am,) I did so as the Dean of Students. I didn't even identify what grade I was representing, and he obviously didn't care (nor did he realize this wasn't the same voice he spoke to less than two days ago.) When I inquired about one Jordache Blue, whose name I deliberately mispronounced, and her questionable grades, I received the following answer, verbatim: "no failure notices were submitted, and even if they were, you know the deal, they want 'em to walk, they walk."

Got that?

The Superintendents want the graduation rates and test scores up, (makes the School Boards feel all warm and fuzzy) so they tell the principals, who tell the vice principals, who tell the Supervisors, who tell the counselors, who tell the teachers, who scream "FOUL" since it's *OUR NAMES* that go on the report card as having "passed" these dull-witted deadbeats on to the cruel world (which is, it should be noted, filled with lawyers dying to sue **us** for "having 'failed' these children.")

You'll notice that the buck—technically—stops at the teachers, but the ones that ultimately get screwed are the kids. Doesn't matter, the "higher ups" are getting what they want. If this was a corporation, these bastards would get arrested for "cooking the books" to hide their financial failures. But hey, *that's* important stuff, like profit margins and stockholders…

this is just our children we're talking about.

Sad but true story #2—1984 in 2013

I'll keep this one short and sour, because I know you've got important things to do, but like a brief but intense winter, it's pretty chilling.

I was asked to sit in on an administrative conference after school (yeah…so much for the "Dean thing" being only one period a day, right?) where we discussed everything from school lunches to state testing. Of course, me being me, I brought up all the stories I had been reading concerning school districts attempting to boycott high stakes testing and students—good, highly intelligent students—flat out refusing to take these tests, and…

I was curtly interrupted (do you sense a theme here?) by a piece of information that, for a moment, silenced even *my* big mouth with its shockingly Orwellian reality. I was informed that in nearby New York, the City Department of Education was, with no remorse, failing students that boycotted state tests. The NYC DOE was *forcing* those students to attend summer school, *even if their teachers recommended that they be promoted* based on their classroom performance.

I could have said "well, we're not New York, are we?" or "doesn't anyone see the hypocrisy in that?" or any number of pithy responses, but the tension in the room was palpable, and I must (embarrassingly) admit that even I play the "shut your mouth and stay employed" game on occasion. This wasn't the forum to play hard ball, and these weren't the people that could do anything about it, even if we all agreed on the only thing I *did* say, under my breath but loud enough that a few heads nodded somberly in agreement:

"Big Brother finally made it into the classroom."

Sad but true story #3—The Perfect Storm

By *week three* of the school year there was a young lady that was already "beyond my jurisdiction" because she had already received TEN disciplinary referrals for MAJOR offenses (from smoking to fighting.) This didn't surprise me *too* much since I had seen her in the hallways pretty frequently, at different times on my travels and, (as any teacher will tell you,) the "hall walkers" are usually the ones you'll see "in the office" at some point.

This lovely young lady, let's call her Elizabeth Bathory, (Liz for short) crossed my path during my lunch period (fortunate) near the front office (fortunate, again) walking the halls (shocking,) with a group of girls, three of which knew me well and respected me (fortunate to the third power.)

I had been meaning to ask Liz what was up with her exponentially growing crime spree, and this was simply too perfect of an opportunity, so...

"Hey Step, what's good?"

"My wife's income."

"You know you miss us!"

"You know I do, ladies. Elizabeth, my dear..."

Liz: *"Me?"*

"You ARE Elizabeth Bathory, yes?"

Liz: (looking to the other girls for back up, all of whom give her the "he's cool" look) *"Yeah."*

"Let me talk to you for a minute."

Liz: *"Oh, I'm on my way to—"*

"Stop. We both know you aren't going to class. Now, let's talk?"

I held the door to the front office open and Liz, smiling, strutted by, compliant but not lacking in confidence. Sigh...Mr. Softie Dean dude loses another lunch period.*

*Do not feel bad for me; I eat more than some small third world countries on most days.

I invited Liz to sit in the empty conference room with me; keeping the door open so the traffic coming and going might keep her at ease, and provide extra ears and eyes for me should things go south. Let me give you a little background on what was sitting across from the table from each other *before* I tell you the outcome of our conversation.

Me: 45 years old, XXL, 25 year teacher alternately loved and feared by students, father of 4 kids, (and step-father of one,) married to the same woman for 29 years, very nice investment portfolio (which I started in my teens), multiple black belts, 400 lb. max bench press, three time published author, Dean of students with an impressive comic book collection and a slight man crush on Dwayne "The Rock" Johnson and I'm going to stop now because it's starting to sound self-congratulatory at this point.

The reason I tell you this is to emphasize the point that the 15 yr.-old girl sitting in front of me *did not give a flying rat's ass about any of that.* She was **staggeringly** unimpressed by me. I think the fact that she was in 8th grade when she became gang affiliated may have had something to do with it, or it may have been the fact that she was living with the third 'relative' since June (it was October 4th,) or perhaps it was the fact that she felt more comfortable telling a complete stranger during our meeting that she was a lesbian prior to informing me that I was only the second adult that knew, and the *first* one was her girlfriend.

Liz was cool, reserved, but no-nonsense in the way that "real" criminals are, (not the loud, posturing stupidity often exhibited by wanna-be tough guys/gals.)

I admired her honesty, when I asked her, point-blank, why she didn't go to class and why she was getting in so much trouble, she said without a fraction of a second's delay that school *didn't mean **** to her and none of these ******* gave a **** about her *** anyway so why the **** should she care. Besides, she was making a ton of money already...*

When I asked her if there were any people in her life worth *not* getting in trouble for, and how they would feel knowing that she was on a fast track to being placed in an alternative program, she looked at me like she was having a hard time believing that I had been working with teens since one million B.C., then she told me that *"Ain't nobody cares, I don't even know my (expletive) father and if I told my Moms I was [uniquely lesbian reference to oral sex] she would [be very upset,] if she gave a [crap.] I got people, I don't sweat these [people] and these teachers and [stuff] 'cause I don't need it; I mean, you alright and all—"*

"Thanks"

"-but they ain't gonna do [anything] 'cause I'm first year so I'm gonna do what I do."

Translation of that last line: School policy dictates that no 9th graders can be expelled or put into the alternative educational placement program without LENGTHY and COSTLY manifestation hearings, a small forest of documentation, etc. no matter how many discipline referrals they receive; therefore, short of killing someone, Elizabeth Bathory knew she would remain walking the halls in between her time disrupting the education of other students and occasionally trying to beat the crap out of/ sell drugs to/ sexually harass some of them.

Pristine logic, I know.

The type of logic that led to my girl Liz getting over EIGHTY-FOUR disciplinary referrals by the time we parted ways for the Summer. Keep in mind, she barely attended class but some…many teachers had stopped writing her up altogether because, (and I am embarrassed to admit this,) our hands were tied by district policy and there really wasn't much we could do.

Just because I was curious, near the end of the year, I called Liz down to Ms. Twister's vice principal's office (which she generously made available for me to do my Dean duties during my "administrative period.") Maybe it was the location, and its traditional implications, maybe it was the accumulated "damage" of a year spent getting reprimanded, punished and (in one case,) arrested, maybe it was something else, but Liz was much colder to me this time. She barely made eye contact, and squirmed and shifted in her seat like a caged animal that just wanted me to finish talking and give her a detention slip, even after I had made it repeatedly clear that I just called her down to talk. Twice, when I paused after speaking to her, she asked *"we done?"*

I thought about sharing the sparse details of our dialogue during this meeting, but I decided not to; I'll only tell you the final exchange. I "play punched" her in the arm and said something like, "Hey, tough girl, I thought you said we were cool?"

"Yeah," looking away with a fast, instantly disappearing smile, *"we cool."*

"Alright," I said, suddenly going from playful and vulnerable to very serious and very sincere (a technique that has worked wonders when dealing with teens, including my own, over the years) "then… look at me, please."

She did, with dead eyes.

"Then know that you can talk to me whenever about whatever, alright? I'm not hard to find."

"Whatever. We done?"

I don't know if the shock and disappointment of my heartfelt offer being dismissed so effortlessly showed on my face, but I have to believe it did. "Yes, ma'am, we're done."

This is what happens when parents, peers, and the school system combine to fail a kid: the perfect storm of absentee parents, poor guardianship (and their poor choices,) and friends/educational policies that only care about what they can *get* from someone.

What about me? Did I fail Elizabeth Bathory?

I don't know, and there will be a tidal wave of new kids coming in September, and I have my kids to deal with every day, so the sad reality is that I don't have the time to dwell on Liz.

But I will.

PART XVII
FREEDOM TO LIVE

No matter what the *stated goal* of any journey, the
true reward is self-knowledge. I think I'll defer to Mr.
Campbell again here, as his description of the "journey's
end" is perfection:

"The individual, through prolonged psychological
disciplines, gives up completely all attachment to his
personal limitations, idiosyncrasies, hopes and fears, no
longer resists the self-annihilation that is prerequisite to
rebirth in the realization of truth, and so becomes ripe,
at last, for the great at-one-ment. His personal ambitions
being totally dissolved, he no longer tries to live but
willingly relaxes to whatever may come to pass in him;
he becomes, that is to say, an anonymity. The law lives in
him with unreserved consent."

(Joseph Campbell *The Hero With A Thousand Faces* 204-205)

What? You want me to try and follow Joseph Campbell?

Yeah, and next I'll be the opening band for KISS, tell Stephen King how
to publish successfully, go to a nude beach with Kate Upton*, tug on
Superman's cape and spit in the wind. Let's just get to the chapter, shall
we?
*Unless, of course, she's up for that. Call me, Kate.

Soundtrack for this chapter: *I'll Stop the World (and Melt With You)*
—Modern English

Get Some Go Again

The title of this chapter, in addition to being a killer Henry Rollins song, is sort of a personal mantra: Find something you want, go after it with relentless energy, work tirelessly to obtain it, and the *minute* you achieve it…find something new, something *harder* to obtain and repeat.

Sound familiar, education people? Bet you never knew you had a rock n' roll mantra, huh?

While I can't say that have *given up* completely *on the limitations, idiosyncrasies and fears* Joseph Campbell mentioned, my journey as a teacher and a parent (and aren't they really the same when you get right down to it?) has diminished them quite a bit.

I love the idea of "being ripe for the great at-one-ment" (Damn, that is a **great** line) and I think most teachers understand what that means—Simply put, our personal success/gratification becomes secondary to that of our kids. I spoke about this briefly in my last book and, at the risk of sounding incredibly pompous, I'm going to quote *myself* for three reasons:

Uno: Based on sales numbers, *nobody read* my second book, so this will be new material to most of you. Ha!

Dos: Many of my students (who have to suffer my relentless lessons on proper citation) said that I have to "quote myself" at some point in this book because it would be hilariously over the top. Your wish is my command!

Tres: Because I believe most of the good teachers out there feel this way.

With that holy trinity of validation in my corner, I give you my current outlook on teaching, as previously stated in *S.C.R.E.W.E.D.*:

> I don't really have dreams of my own anymore…I live, for intents and purposes, for the dreams of [our] kids. I think that makes me a very effective teacher. I think I'm not alone in that respect. …I work with my kids like my life depends on it because it *does*. I would be lying if I denied the fact that the chance to help [our] kids realize their dreams is the only thing that gets me out of bed most days… You want me teaching your kids, you really do.
>
> (Stepnowski 239-240)

Well THAT was weird, but it certainly applies to the theme of this, the lesson learned from our heroic journey to self-realization; at the very least, it sounded a **lot** like *"personal ambitions being totally dissolved…no longer tr[ying] to live but willingly relax[ing] to whatever may come to pass in him…,"* right?

Teaching, this profession we have chosen, unlike just about any other, forces you to break off pieces of yourself and trim your selfish aspirations until not much is left but your will and the fact that most of it will be dedicated to the offspring of complete strangers, many of whom will oppose your attempts to better the world they live in by bettering their children, often in spite of a system that is set up to impede their progress in the first place.

I think I can keep it real with you; you've spent hours of your valuable time with me here, so we're cool like that now. Teaching has become, as I said before, parenting with a paycheck, mentoring with benefits, etc. From the most basic elementary classrooms to the most brain-melting graduate classes, teachers are expected to handle the type of confrontation, display the type of compassion, and endure the type of scrutiny usually associated with parenthood, but unlike parents—**we** do this under the microscope.

FULL FRONTAL HONESTY ALERT! I'm a parent. I love my kids. I love my kids with the continual awareness that they may not be here tomorrow…

and I still want to abuse them from time to time.

Go ahead, tell me I'm terrible, tell me I'm a bad dad; tell me I'm some kind of knuckle-dragging Neanderthal who (insert horrified voice) *condones hurting children.*

For those of you who think that, I will assume one of the following:

You don't have kids, in which case I care about as much about your opinion as LeBron James cares about your criticism of his perimeter defense.

You aren't *involved enough* in a kid's life to experience the kind of frustration that comes with being in constant contact with someone a generation or more removed from you.

You're in total denial of your own occasional abusive impulses, or

you're a better person than me—in which case, I am in awe of your restraint and character.

For those of you who are neither exceptional, nor judgmental, I know you sympathize with the ever surging tsunami of conflicting emotions that come from being involved in a kid's life. Now I want those of you who ARE all too aware of the emotional toll of active parenting to imagine *every move you make with your child(ren) being **observed, reviewed, critiqued** and **criticized.***

I'll give you a minute to think about that.

ALL the things you say, ALL the things you do, EVERY activity you plan—all subject to public scrutiny.

Welcome, my friend, to the daily reality of the contemporary teacher.

But I'm here to give you some good news. I'm here to tell you, *teachers* of children, *parents* of those children, *citizens* who have to live in the world inherited **by** these children, and the *children* themselves, that the journey is the important part, not the destination. Oh, and guess what? We are ALL together on this journey.

The world is shrinking; this is a global economy now, and people worldwide will come to depend upon one another sooner than later, and—contrary to the expectations and analysis of the education "reformers" and career politicians/administrators that promote all this testing and emotionless, one-size-fits-all instruction—the END, the score, the "lexile number," the diploma, whatever you want to call it *isn't* the important part,

the *human element* IS.

And I, for one, have come to embrace that truth here, at the end of [this particular part of] my journey.

Campbell tells us that, to earn the "freedom to live," the hero must *"no longer resist the self-annihilation that is prerequisite to rebirth in the realization of truth, and [he]becomes ripe, at last, for the great at-one-ment"* (Campbell 204).

I'm getting closer. I, along with many of my brothers and sisters in the profession, have come to grips with the fact that self-destruction is a beautifully unfortunate part of doing our job well. I don't mean self-annihilation in an *Ozzy Osbourne-dear-lord-how-the-heck-are-you-still-alive?* sort of way, of course; I mean the 100% giving of your energies to the improvement of others, the total submission to devoting oneself to those you were charged to protect, even if they fight you kicking and screaming all the way.

Campbell further informs us that only this type of dedication can prepare us for the ultimate realization of the truth, what he calls the great at-one-ment—which I find to be the realization that, ahem, *we are ALL together on this journey.*

I used to tell my wife, when we argued and she accused me of trying to "sabotage" her or "turn the kids against her" that—at least in that instance—she was incorrect and being irrational. "What purpose would it serve," I would ask, "to bash the head of the other person in the kayak as we tried to navigate the rapids of having children? All that would do is make more work for *me* and exponentially increase the chances of *failure!*"

I wasn't kidding then and I'm not kidding now. In my jobs as both a teacher and a parent, I will correct some things, criticize many things, and question *everything,* but I will never do it in a destructive way simply because it would make no sense, given that—and you may have heard this before—***we are ALL together on this journey.***

And I need your help.

And there it is—the freedom I was searching for on this particular leg of my journey.

I have to learn to breathe though the hard parts,

the *I-could-be making-a-lot-more-money-doing-something-less-soul-crushing* moments,

the *why-does-it-seem-as-if-everyone-is-against-me moments,*

the *will-this-ever-end-before-I-finally-snap-and-lose-everything-I've-worked-for* moments because,

in order—you **could**, they **aren't**, and it **will**.

But even if it seems as though you couldn't, they are, and it won't—those moments are *life*. That's what life looks like, and only by looking at it in perspective do we survive to fight the good fight another day.

You can do it.

Cultivate the help of the parents that want to help and *help them help you.* As for the parents that don't do anything but spout venom at you because they're posturing to hide their obvious shortcomings? They have their own demons to battle; let them be and don't burn yourself out trying to expand the vision of people that *want* to be blind.

Find people "up the food chain" that care about the kids (They're out there, believe me; in shorter and shorter supply, but they're out there) and develop honest, working relationships with them. I know it's hard to trust administrators when so many of them are…well, you know, but you have to trust others if you're going to survive this gig and do it well. I just admitted (a few pages ago!) that I needed help and I'm as alpha-male as there is, so I did it; you can do it, too. And you can—and will—do it because it will help you do what you went into this job in the first place to do,

educate and evolve our children.

Speaking, at last, of the kids—our kids. They are *our* kids, you know?

You know.

You also know, but sometimes forget, that *that one kid,* the one that tells you in June, maybe the following year, maybe years later, that you changed his/her life; that they would have never (insert amazing, life-changing accomplishment) without you…

That's a HUMAN LIFE, and you changed it, profoundly and forever.

A **HUMAN LIFE**: EVOLVED, IMPROVED, HAPPIER, SMARTER, and MORE SELF-SUFFICIENT because of YOU. What else is there, I ask you?

The kids are smarter than we think, more resilient than they know, and they can handle the truth a hell of a lot better than most of the world gives them credit for. Be honest with them, teach them as you would your own, and understand, if you do this job right, with all your heart and soul, that,

say it with me—

Teaching sucks, but we love it.

The End
(of *this* journey, anyway.)

An Apology: The Most Important Chapter I Will Ever Write.

If I never publish another book, write another chapter, at least I will have done this; and that will be enough.

I am sorry.

I apologize to every student I have even taught, including, and most painfully of all, my own children, to whom I provided the very first rudiments of education. I have, far too often, allowed a concept of "education" that was foreign to my own dictate my actions, oftentimes to your detriment.

To clarify: I understand, better than most, that I work for an antiquated system, a system of public education that tells **millions** of kids <u>every year</u> that what *they* are good at isn't important. Our educational system is a totally outdated relic, *created* during a time when it worked, but was **never significantly changed**, even as the world, its economy, its technology, its people hurtled forward. To quote Sir Ken Robinson, "[We're] trying to meet the future by doing what [we] were doing in the past." And yet, I have been guilty of playing into that lie, and hurting my kids and students in the process.

I know I've done it, I've apologized to my kids (ALL of 'em) for doing it, but—somehow—getting it down on paper made it real and it exposes me for the hypocrite I have been.

I am ashamed of what I have done.

I've put report cards on the refrigerator, fostering competition among my own children, for grades in subjects that are largely irrelevant, some of which are taught by people who should have retired many years ago, *some* of whom should never have been teachers in the *first place*.

All the while, I've dismissed their *unique* talents, choosing to berate them about keeping rooms clean and Spanish 2 grades up while virtually ignoring the things that truly matter and will, ironically, make them successes in the "real world," whatever the hell *that* means.

And so, if you'll permit me a moment, I'd like to apologize to my kids, and my students.

Samantha, your time volunteering has transformed you. Tutoring kids that needed help, and dealing with the frustration that comes from having them lash out at you, because you're the only one that *cared*, forged a strength within you that very few people your age can claim. Your work with the elderly, who so desperately need to be heard, has given you an appreciation of our world and expanded your horizons beyond anything you could have learned in schools; and your work with dementia patients, even though it is often frustrating and terrifying, has proved, beyond a shadow of a doubt, that you are a dynamic force of compassion and strength in an increasingly selfish, weakening world. I'm sorry that I complain about driving you to these things when I should be telling you how unbelievably proud I am of you. The self-confidence you have forged by overcoming so many adversities has made you the woman you are. You chose a nice young man who respects you and you are able to look adults in the eye because you have the self-confidence that comes from having DONE it and not just dreamed it. You will succeed in whatever you set your mind to because of the intangibles that you acquired outside anything I may have taught you. Because you are my oldest living child, because you are my only daughter, because you followed Cain, because of so many things, I have been **relentless** in my demands from you, but only because I am in awe of what you can withstand, and how you turn adversity into amazing. Your potential is truly limit-less—live up to it.

Mason, you have always had the rarest combination of abilities in a boy your age—the sublime strength needed to be compassion-ate to those younger than you, the ability (for the most part) to avoid the peer pressure of those close to your age, and a natural ease with those who are your seniors. Your work ethic, when it comes to physi-cal labor, is jaw-dropping in its consistency. You've always had your mother's gift for being able to visualize projects completed before the first nail was hammered; that, combined with your natural abil-ity to learn how to bring those visions to fruition are amazing to me. I have always made you feel less than adequate for your occasional bad grades, hurting your feelings more times than I care to admit, all the while ignoring the fact that you, more than any single individual, have been responsible for Brendan's transformation, and neither I, nor he, will ever be able to thank you enough for that. Your abilities have, from time to time, manifested themselves in arrogance, but I know that it will mellow to self-confidence, and your heart is pure, so I anxiously look forward to what you will do to better this ever-disappointing world with your unique skill set, very little of which was forged by doing busy work and passing tests in school. There are many types of intelligences, and I'm sorry I didn't acknowledge yours more often. There is greatness within you, son. As I have told you so many times—become who you were *born* to be.

Frankie, my namesake; from the time you were little, you were a virtually no maintenance child that evolved into a self-sufficient young man. You have always been exceptional in school, not because you mindlessly followed the herd, but because you never lost the joy of learning new things. Please don't ever lose that, son. Your physical skills are the stuff of local legend—your speed, power, strength and (most importantly,) humility and unselfishness make me proud that you share my name before you ever laced a cleat or put on a glove. Beyond the world of school and sports, you have been forced to witness and endure far too many things at your young age alone in the company of only your own thoughts. As much as it hurts me that you sometimes prefer to suffer in silence—I see the iron resolve that it has forged within you. Know that it is not the "straight As" that define you, it is the thirst for knowledge, and the desire to honor the family name that *led* to those grades that sets you apart from your peers. Navigate your teen years wisely, ever cognizant that unique does not mean weird, it means unique. I am anxious to see what the perfect storm of athletics, altruism and athletics produces, and know that I am always here for you on your journey.

All three of you—As much as it kills me that you don't really need me anymore, (and that may be why I continually find things to yell at you about, to hang on to the remnants of being "Dad,") you **have given me the relief that every parent dreams of, knowing that "they'll be ok without me"** at a very, very young age, and I love you all for that more than words on a page can ever hope to express.

Brendan, maybe no other kid has ever had to endure my high expectations, Spartan discipline and righteous rage in such concentrated form. I know it's very easy to get the impression that I don't like you, and I would totally understand if you don't like me very much, but—as time passes—I think you'll grow to see that I was doing my very best to erase the damage done to you by people that didn't care enough to do the "dirty work" involved in parenting. I am very proud of you and how quickly you were able to adapt to life as a "Step child"—no easy feat, young man—and no matter how much I yell, punish, and correct, please know that I only do it because I *care* enough to place high expectations upon you.

I can't promise that I won't hurt any of your feelings by defining you by your report cards again; it's pretty deep in my hard drive at this point and it might take a while; but I *can* promise to balance my obsession with your scholastic performance with what is really important—like keeping your rooms clean.

See, I told you it might take a while.

Finally, to my students, (and you are *always* my students, even if you left my classroom decades ago)—if I've EVER had you in my class, chances are I've screwed up. I don't work with a net and I sure as hell don't follow any "standard curriculum," so I have tried a lot of things that sounded great in my head but crashed like the Hindenburg in class. I can only hope that within that mountain of magnificent failures, a few magic moments of inspiration erupted. I worked past the point of exhaustion looking for stuff that was new and exciting that would stretch your minds, open your eyes, and break you free from the shackles of what passes for "education" in this country. I have always told, and will continue to tell, every student I have ever taught that the highest compliment I could ever pay them was to treat them as I treat my own children.

I have, and I know that sometimes that hurt. But I did it because I loved you enough to *try*, so please, forgive my indiscretions and teaching mistakes, they were all done with no regard for my status, job security, or financial well-being—I have done everything, EVERYTHING I can to make you *think for yourself* and become *better than me*, and I'm sorry for every bullcrap benchmark, standardized test and/or district-mandated assignment that I subjected you to when you *knew* I didn't believe in them. You deserve better.

Parents, you have trusted me with your most prized possessions: flesh of your flesh, blood of your blood, and I have always, ALWAYS done my very best, in every circumstance, to teach your children the way I would my own. If that's not good enough for you, I don't know what to tell you.

I mentioned Cain, my oldest son, who was taken from me when he was only a few weeks old. I made my son a promise that I would live with relentless intensity, squeezing two lifetimes into the time frame of one, to honor the years and years that were stolen from him. I only realize (as I purge some of these demons on paper) that I screwed *that* up, too—allowing myself to become bitter and fixated on minutiae in the pursuit of staying busy, sometimes simply for the sake of staying busy. I am sorry, son; know that I am working so very hard to make you proud of me, and to keep my promise to you.

I'll get this teaching/parenting thing right, sooner than later, I promise.

Famous Last Words
(...no, seriously, this is the last chapter).

Since I started writing this book, quite a few things have happened in the world of American education that, while directly related to the source material in this book, would probably disturb the continuity of the chapters if I just went back and "dropped them in" at the end.

Yes, I just said "source material" and "continuity of the chapters." I must be gettin' close to being an O-fish-ul author-type-person!

Nah, probably not.

The reality is that, every day, I am besieged (in a good way) by anecdotes and articles, hyperlinks and hyperbole, Facebook posts and Twitter feeds, Emails, texts, letters and newspaper clippings that have convinced me that the aforementioned "source material" will remain relevant long after this book finds its way into a 451 degree oven, and that's as comforting to me as an author as it is terrifying to me as a teacher.

As much as I wanted to include everything about teaching that the general public doesn't "get" in this book, I simply couldn't do it. So if I left out something that you feel was important, I do apologize; but trying to fit all the ills of modern compulsory schooling into one book was like Dante trying to figure out how to punish every type of sinner in one epic poem.

Hmmmm… Note to self: Consider *Step's Edferno*, (wherein people that are ruining education in this country are explicitly NAMED and TORTURED in a variety of graphic methods) as possible fourth book.

Oh yeah…like you *wouldn't* want to see (insert name of person you were thinking of) getting their heads "sharpened" in a giant pencil sharpener to be used over and over for all eternity on one constantly reproducing standardized test for the Demons of the Malebolge.

Fourth book fantasies aside, we all know that teaching is no different than any other profession: If done properly, consistently, over time—the people doing it will think it sucks, that the people they work with are idiots, that the money they earn isn't worth the sacrifices they make, that nobody understands what they're going through (except maybe those in the profession,) and that something, ANYthing would be better than this…

Sound familiar?

I know. I hear it from everyone from my kids' dental hygienists to my brother-in-law and his partners in the law firm to the guys that winterize my sprinkler system to the girl at the counter at 7-11…

That having been said, this whole book started with the premise that, for some reason, non-teacher personnel all over America think that they know what it is to be a teacher.

You don't.

Moreover, people seem to think that, if their current job didn't work out, that they could always "go into teaching" and do the job properly if they had to.

You couldn't.

Of course, it doesn't help that the mass media makes it seem like teaching is something you could do with a three month crash course and few box tops from participating breakfast cereals.

It isn't.

We never get the "white collar" respect that doctors, lawyers, engineers, accountants, and architects get; but we never get the "blue collar" street credibility that builders, mechanics, plumbers, and trash men get, either! Nor do we get the love that the creative community—the artists, musicians, authors and singers get.

Trust me, we build, we heal, we crunch numbers, we design and we (occasionally) take out the trash. Oh, and by the way…

Who do you think *TAUGHT* **the doctors, lawyers, engineers, accountants, architects, builders, mechanics, plumbers, trash men, artists, musicians, authors, singers AND EVERY OTHER PROFESSION COME TO THINK OF IT to do what they do?!?!**

Because I'm a perfectionist idiot with mild OCD and a sense of fate, I was looking for some sort of *sign* (beyond my editor telling me he wouldn't read another page and my publisher threatening to forget my name) that this book was "Done" with a capital D.

Ask and ye shall receive.

I was sitting on the beach yesterday (Saturday, July 6th) with my wife and she directed my attention to one of those prop planes that pulls an advertisement behind it. The pilot was making passes over the sands of the New Jersey Shore, and the advertisement said NOW HIRING TEACHERS, with a website like TeachNow.org or some crap like that, I couldn't really see at that point because my vision had gone red.

As usual, Dr. Dawn's sarcasm snapped me out of my homicidal impulses and put things in perspective: *"Hey, that teaching thing must be easy, why don't you try* ***that****?"*

I glared. She smiled. I smiled.

"Yeah, sounds easy, *everybody* should give it a shot."

Good luck with that.

—Frank Stepnowski 7/7/2013

Acknowledgments

I'm not, nor do I think I will ever be, a big time professional author; therefore my books, and any success they enjoy, are a collaborative effort on the part of too many people to mention, but some individuals I simply must mention (because they paid me, threatened to beat me up, or offered me sex, food, or iTunes cards...)

This book started as a VERY large group of files, which then became a VERY large pile of papers, all of which needed a tremendous amount of editing. Turning my angry, oft-profane rants into a grammatically correct, mass-market acceptable, coherent book became the Sisyphean task of my symbiotic aide de camp, **Ed Trautz.** I gave this newly married young man the impossible task of telling me what to keep, what to add, what to change, and asked him to do it all without regard for my feelings and without expectation of payment. You *wish* you had a friend liked Ed Trautz, and I do. Remember that name, folks, and get his autograph now before you have to wait in line and pay for it.

My second book, *S.C.R.E.W.E.D., An Educational Fairytale* was published in 2011, amazingly, on March 7th—my late son's birthday. That moment of beautiful serendipity could never have happened without the help of **Tommy Castagna**, graphic design guru, formatting wizard, and cover designer extraordinaire. Tommy took time away from his beautiful wife and children to ensure that this book was formatted properly, had an awesome cover, and got to the publisher's office on time.

Mike Dillon unselfishly offered to take the "author photo" that you see on the back of the book. You simply have no idea how much work went into that simple image. Suffice it to say that he made *me* look good, and I believe the staff now refers to him as "Miracle Mike" because of this. That picture, along with the cover and the editing, created a book that was a clearly evolved product from the first two.

Every Dark Knight has to have a Lucius Fox behind the scenes to ensure that the expensive toys run properly, and my tech support ALWAYS comes in the form of **Bill Hubbard:** childhood friend, expert on all things computer-related, and one of the truly good guys in this world. Thankfully, Bill made time in between setting up corporate accounts and un-freezing my Mom's computer (again) to make sure my laptop runs with frightening precision and speed.

I begged **Frank Wilson**, a man who has made all the rounds there are to make in the literary world, to give a local, self-published author a book review. He said "no, I want to do a full interview and an online chat as well." Our interview, in his South Philadelphia home, happened on the day of an *Earthquake,* and that [literal] earth shaking experience was dwarfed by the feeling I had seeing that full page interview, (with a truly awesome illustration) in a major newspaper, *The Philadelphia Inquirer*. That made me feel like a "real" author, and I can never thank you enough for that.

Speaking of coverage, I have to thank **Tommy & Marianne Milligan** and **Kathy Westfield** from *The Spirit*, **Thomas Waring** from *The Northeast Times* and *The Wire*, **Tara Gillespie** from *The Penndian,* the vivacious **Cary Nadzak** from *Looneyteachr.com*, as well as *Southeast*

Jersey Magazine and *TeachHub*.com for helping get the word out about the books.

I sent **John Merrow,** BIG TIME broadcast journalist who has reported on education issues for more than three decades, a Twitter request to autograph my *seriously* "notated" copy of his book, *Below C Level*; I got a personalized book, a feature on his *Learning Matters* website, a wave of new Twitter followers, and the friendship of a man I have always respected as an advocate for teachers. Thank you, John.

I donated a lot of the profits from *S.C.R.E.W.E.D.* to the Wounded Warriors Project because I understand that freedom isn't free, and the men and women that serve to protect that freedom deserve every respect I can afford them. One of those brave men, **Larry Leissner,** and his **Pennsylvania Air & Army National Guard's 3rd Police Operational Mentor and Liaison Team,** honored my small contribution to their enormous effort by flying a flag [in honor of my late son, Cain,] above their active military base in Afghanistan. I look at that flag every day.

Of course, I must give love to **The Avengers**, my inner circle of dearest friends: You already heard about (Iron Man) **Ed Trautz** and (Black Widow) **Dr. Dawn**, now meet the rest of the crew:

- (Nick Fury) **Fred Roth** and (The Scarlet Witch) **Akima Morgan,** two of the most selfless, beautiful people I have ever had the pleasure to call friends. All they do is give, never asking for anything but love in return.
- (Black Panther) **Bobby Ellis,** the silence behind the violence, one of the smartest men I know. Mr. Ellis has been a Godsend to me and my family on more occasions then I dare to count.
- (Thor) **Billy Staab,** my brother from another mother and partner in healthy diet, heavy metal, and happy kids. Billy has always been there, and always will be.
- (The Hulk) **Pete Nardello,** reminds me daily that there is true

power in compassion; my first children's book will be dedicated to your beautiful Anna Rose.

- (Hawkeye) **Marc Granieri,** a singular man of impeccable character and iron-bound honor; if all I ever got out of working at (our place of employment) was your friendship, that would have been more than enough.

You read all about **Tanisha Crawford** and the "Teacher All Star." That night was sweet, sweet vindication for a quarter century of doing the right thing; Tanisha, you gave me, my friends and family a memory that will live forever, and I will always love you for that.

Maira Diaz, and her wonderful staff at the Pennsauken Public Library, welcomed a controversial lightning rod into her author's roundtable, providing me with invaluable contacts and inspiration to get writing again. Maira's family, staff, and building, are a testament to her quiet dignity and strength.

Loud love to all the **Badass teachers** (*check out The Badass teachers association on Facebook!)* out there for spreading the "gospel according to Step" on Facebook, Twitter, Pinterest and other media venues: **April Estep, Robyn Barberry, Gene Steinmann, Patti Donato-Frische, Nicole Vitale, Gavin West, Kathy Zorianski Ungvarsky, Julie Bardelli Clark, Bill O'Hanlon, Lynn Holland Reading, Maura Harbison, Kani Ellis Fields, Kristi Gibboney Dojack, Kate Laskowski, Austin Green, Maria Manzo-Hotchkiss** and **the legions of "STEPchildren."**

Same goes to the **"original fans"**—**Molly Stepnowski** and **Colleen S. Grazione**—that set up the *Fans of the Author Frank Stepnowski* page on Facebook before we knew how this would all turn out.

Props must be paid to **Dad** and **Mom,** the alpha and the omega of my relentless drive for self-improvement and voracious appetite for the written word. Don't blame them, folks, anything *decent* about me probably came from them.

Last, but by no means least, **to each and every person who took the time to selflessly promote my books** (via the internet, social media and word of mouth.) Your time is valuable, and the fact that you took some of it to help spread the word makes me want to shake every one of your hands in person. I'm not kidding when I say I appreciate *every single one of you*.

Donations to the Wounded Warrior project

One does not accept the nickname "Captain America" from his friends and take it lightly. Freedom is not free, and I am happy to fight for, pay for, and protect it. With that in mind, I am proud to say that a portion of the proceeds from my books gets donated to the Wounded Warriors Project, a non-profit organization that provides tangible support for wounded service and men and women and helps them on the road to healing, both physically and mentally.

For more information, check out **www.woundedwarriorproject.org**

About the Voice.

Frank Stepnowski is, with the exception of the legions of people responsible for everything decent he's ever done, a completely self-sufficient organism with a keen sense of irony. He enjoys loud music, offensive literature, functional fitness, and long walks with his pot-bellied pig Napoleon, whom he has not yet purchased, but hopes to do so with the sales of this book.

Until Step and swine find each other, you can engage him—the author, not the pig—in witty conversation on **Facebook:** *Frank Stepnowski* or *Fans of the Author Frank Stepnowski* or on **Twitter** @ *Frankstep1*.

*"O you of sturdy intellects/ Observe the teachings hidden here/ Beneath the veil of verses so obscure—Dante Aligheri **Inferno** IX: 61-63*

A final note on editing:

I'm not sure what the length of this book will be, once the publishers do their thing; but I *can* tell you that a 504-page WORD document fraught with errors in grammar, spelling, punctuation and *judgment* got whittled down to a 299-page proof thanks to seemingly endless days/hours of editing AFTER I'm done being a father, husband, stepfather, teacher, babysitter, coach, provider, landscaper, spider smusher, etc...

It is no secret that my first book went out with a few mistakes and a couple of typographical errors. I haven't heard about any errors in the second book, but I'm sure there may be one or two. I have learned to enlist the help of others, but I am still a self-published guy who writes books without the editorial assistance of a major publishing company that real authors get.

So, needless to say, I make mistakes; and <u>any mistakes in this book are my own</u>, and are my fault exclusively.

CPSIA information can be obtained at www.ICGtesting.com
Printed in the USA
BVOW03s2026220415

397206BV00002B/260/P